THE DECISION IS YOURS

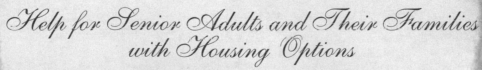

Help for Senior Adults and Their Families with Housing Options

P. DAVID JAKES

LifeWay Press
Nashville, Tennessee

The Decision Is Yours

7800-03
ISBN 0-8054-9877-X

Dewey Decimal Classification: 362.6
Subject Heading: ELDERLY - CARE

Printed in the United States of America

Illustrations by Laura Tedeschi

LifeWay Press
127 Ninth Avenue, North
Nashville, Tennessee 37234

CONTENTS

ACKNOWLEDGMENTS

To my wife, Donna, and daughter, Laura, whose patience, understanding, and support encouraged me and allowed me to devote a large amount of time to writing this book.

To my mother, Maxine C. Jakes, who suffered a cerebral vascular accident (stroke) during the writing of this book, and who through the years has utilized many of the housing and health care options and services mentioned herein. The contents of this book were helpful to me as I faced important decisions relating to her care and treatment.

To the residents and clients of campuses and services affiliated with Arizona Baptist Retirement Centers, whose inspiration and encouragement have been a lasting influence on my life, creating a sincere desire to identify unmet needs of senior adults and to seek new methods of ministry to them.

To the members of the Leadership Committee and Management Staff of Arizona Baptist Retirement Centers, whose input, assistance, and guidance were invaluable during the planning, creating, and writing process.

David Jakes
Summer, 1995

PREFACE

Senior Adult Trends and Challenges

America is experiencing a massive demographic shift to a society of mature adults. Baby boomers, those born between 1946 and 1964, are moving into senior adulthood. Ken Dychtwald, in his book, *Age Wave*, (Jeremy P. Tarcher, Inc., 1989) predicted that this change in age demographics will not only affect our society, but will cause us to rethink our goals, purposes, and challenges of life in its various stages.

Two factors are causing the senior adult population increase: 1) healthier lifestyles along with advances in medical technology are extending life expectancy, and 2) the baby boomers are aging. In 1990, some 2.2 million people celebrated their 65th birthday; that's 6,000 per day! Dychtwald's studies show that by the year 2025, there will be more than 66 million older persons. People over 65 years of age will outnumber teenagers two to one.

This increasingly mature society is creating new trends by changing the way we think about senior adulthood.

Medical technology continues to discover new methods and drugs for keeping Americans alive longer and making them healthier and more active. According to the Census Bureau, in 1776 the life expectancy of the average American was 34 years. In 1886 that number grew to 40. Statistics now show life expectancy extends to 75 years. By 2040, men are predicted to live 86 years and women are predicted to live about 91.5 years. By 2020, approximately 300,000 Americans will be 100 years old or more, compared to 50,000 in 1993.

Churches and other religious organizations working with senior adults are facing this challenge—what some call "the graying of America." But are they responding to all of its implications? And if they are, is the response quick enough, and is it effective?

How will the churches and other organizations address the vast and varied needs of senior adults? Will they provide housing and health care for these senior adults? How will they minister to their needs? What guidance and direction will these older adults receive?

These are probing questions. Some answers are found in this book. There are those who need guidance in the decisions relating to retirement housing and health care. The purpose of this book is to provide some measure of understanding about the housing and health care industry in order to help you make the choices that are right for you or for some senior adult you love.

Today's trends give us a glimpse into tomorrow's reality. As a country and as a Christian community, we need to realize that our goals and purposes are changing with a maturing society, presenting new challenges and redefining the way we will live.

Background of This Book

During 23 years in health care management, I have watched individuals make crucial housing and health care decisions. Some have made excellent choices. Others have made poor choices, resulting in undesirable outcomes. This has been particularly true of housing and health care choices made by senior adults and their family members.

Why? Because these decisions are often made under stressful and emotional conditions when an immediate need or a health condition requires an immediate decision. Objectivity under these conditions is never easy.

I always have felt there should be a guide for making such important decisions, a guide simple enough for uninformed persons to understand and comprehensive enough to enable them to evaluate the facts before they make key decisions. This guide should gather available resources and explain them so they can be quickly accessed in a particular situation and evaluated for making needed decisions. I've tried to provide you and your family a guide just like I've described.

Intended Audience

The Decision Is Yours starts with the assumption that a decision needs to be made regarding retirement housing and health care for senior adults. Therefore, the targeted audience is senior adults making those decisions. However, grown children, relatives, and friends of senior adults will find the book helpful as they plan for their own future and as they assist their parents, grandparents, and other relatives.

How to Read This Book

The purpose and challenge of *The Decision Is Yours* is to help you develop the knowledge and skills to make the right decision in a given situation. The book does not offer a "one-size-fits-all" or "cookie-cutter" approach, but rather guides you through the process of making the decisions.

Help in your decision-making process is only a chapter away! In Chapter 1, "Making The Right Decision," you'll find a step-by-step approach for assessing your individual needs by answering a series of questions regarding ability to perform the activities of daily living. Depending on your answers to these questions, the book refers you to a specific chapter or chapters that deal with the key issues you surface to help you assess those issues and make important choices.

While it will be helpful to read all the chapters, you can skip sections and chapters that do not address your immediate situation.

I suggest that you read carefully Chapter 2 and refer to it as needed. It contains a glossary of terms to help you understand the housing and health care industry, especially since these terms are not used consistently throughout this country.

Overview of the Contents

The book is divided into four sections and provides an overview of the retirement housing and health care delivery system for senior adults. Section 1 consists of three chapters dealing with self-care and caregiving. For most senior adults, these chapters will help you to assess your needs and access the services to enable you to remain in a home setting and be as independent as possible.

Section 2 consists of four chapters concerning retirement housing options. The primary focus of these chapters is explaining the various services and levels of housing provided in retirement centers. You'll find guidelines for evaluating different levels of care and a practical understanding and overview of the retirement housing industry.

Section 3 consists of seven chapters dealing with nursing home care. You may not be currently considering this option; still, it will be helpful to read this section for its practical guides in planning for, choosing, and dealing with nursing home admission or placement.

Finally, Section 4 consists of four chapters explaining alternative health care and specialized services, such as home health care, hospice care, and Alzheimer's care. Included is a chapter that promotes Christian care as a significant ministry to senior adults.

As you begin to read this book, remember that each chapter offers you the opportunity to assess daily living skills and to understand the retirement housing and health care available to senior adults. You know better than anyone else your specific needs and the decisions you are facing. In the end, the decision is really yours based upon your own best judgment, understanding, and insight. If this book provides some guidance and insight, your reward will be worth the reading. And my reward will be in knowing you have been helped.

INTRODUCTION
DECISIONS! DECISIONS! DECISIONS!

Maxine was a 79-year-old widow who made her home in an independent living apartment on the campus of a retirement center. Her health had been deteriorating over the past year, and she was becoming more feeble. Due to increases in medical and prescription costs, her financial resources were being depleted. Maxine and her two sons faced a critical decision regarding whether Maxine needed a more supervised environment that would provide three nutritious meals per day, daily monitoring of medications, and assistance with activities of daily living. Her financial resources were limited, and her two sons could not provide caregiving in their homes due to work requirements and extensive travel. Maxine and her sons faced an important decision—how best to meet her needs.

What resources can meet Maxine's health and safety needs?

Tom and Karen had provided care to her 90-year-old father, Mitch, for the past two years. After his wife died, Mitch required considerable supervision, care, and companionship, which was straining Tom and Karen's marriage relationship. Mitch's health had deteriorated to the point that Karen could not physically handle the care he required, nor could she handle the emotional stress of caregiving in her home. Tom and Karen began to seek other options. As they visited various nursing homes, they quickly became frustrated because they did not know how to select the appropriate facility, how to qualify for financial support, or how to select a physician to take care of Mitch.

What resources will assist Tom and Karen in their important decision?

Bob and Carolyn were in their senior years living about 1,400 miles from their middle-aged, married children. They were moderately independent, but relied on each other for some care and limited support. As time passed, they realized they should seek external resources to provide the support they needed. Bob and Carolyn began to explore community agencies that could provide assistance and support within their home, but they did not know where to start their search.

What services were available to enable Bob and Carolyn to remain independent in their own home?

Mildred was a 76-year-old widow who had lived in her home for 37 years. Her house had 2,800 square feet with two stories and four bedrooms. It was becoming increasingly difficult for her to perform the daily housekeeping and maintenance chores. She felt unsafe in her deteriorating neighborhood, but did not want to leave her home and move to a strange place. As she began to research her options, she decided to move to a retirement center. However, there were so many different types of centers: those with apartments only, assisted living, residential care, and continuum of care retirement centers with multiple levels of care. Several years prior, she had visited several centers with a friend. However, she did not pay much attention because she was not old enough then to move to a retirement center and was in relatively good health. She wished for some community resources to help her choose wisely from the various retirement housing options.

Where could Mildred obtain the advice she needed?

Ted was a 73-year-old male who had been diagnosed with cancer three years before. As time passed, his cancer spread into other organs, and his physician had ordered hospice care for his remaining months. He did not want to be institutionalized, but rather to spend his next few months at home with his immediate family. Ted knew he and his family would need emotional support through this ordeal, but did not know anything about hospice care or the different agencies providing this type of medical service.

How could his decision be facilitated at such an important time?

Maxine, Tom and Karen, Bob and Carolyn, Mildred, and Ted had one thing in common. They all had to make important decisions about various options regarding retirement housing and health care. Each of these individuals faced a decision they were not prepared to make. They had no knowledge or skills to assist them in their decision making. They did not know the important questions to ask, where to go to acquire the needed resources, or how to rank their choices and options to discover the best outcome for them and their families.

I have written this book to assist individual senior adults and their family members in choosing the best options regarding self-care, caregiving, retirement housing, nursing home care, and various alternative health care services.

I know these decisions are difficult, for they are usually made during a stressful situation where emotions are raw and tender. Small wonder that most families wait until there is insufficient time to make better decisions.

The title of this book, *The Decision Is Yours*, is appropriate because the decision really IS YOURS! The most important aspect of any decision is researching all the variables and knowing all the facts so that your decision is intelligent, informed, and objective. The decision really is yours if you are aware of and act on these important elements:

- You do not wait until time is limited.

- You know the external resources and services available.

- You know the right questions to ask.

- You know where to go to find answers to those questions.

- You know how to cut through the inevitable red tape.

- You know what to expect of agencies and institutions.

- You know the usual time required to implement your decisions.

- You make decisions in an objective manner.

- You know the financial resources available.

- You know how to easily assess your circumstances and situation.

- You know how to access the health care delivery system.

Through the years, I have seen hundreds of senior adults make poor choices they never would have made had they properly planned ahead and clearly understood their options. As I reflect upon some of these poor decisions, it is apparent that many were based on emotion, lack of knowledge, no assistance, poor health, lack of objectivity, geographic restrictions, and financial limitations. Even worse, such decisions resulted in depleting financial resources, disrupting families and marriages, substandard care, and shorter lives.

Unfortunately, many people wait until it is too late to gather the information needed to make sensible choices that can produce the right decision.

Making the right decision and being in control of the process is the heart and purpose of this book. I trust you will benefit from the information and guidance provided and find the book a source of encouragement, strength, and assistance in facilitating those decisions with such far-reaching effects.

SECTION 1
SELF-CARE AND CAREGIVING

CHAPTER 1
MAKING THE RIGHT DECISION

Self-care, caregiving, retirement housing, or nursing home care? These decisions are no more difficult to make than other decisions. However, most people do not take the time to explore or research their options. They often wait until the last minute and let circumstances dictate the decision. If you do that, the decision will not be yours!

Identifying your needs and the services to meet those needs is the first step in making the right decision. You can take that step now by looking at the extent to which health problems or disabilities interfere with your independence—that is, your ability to care for yourself in routine activities of daily life.

These activities include: mobility; eating; bathing; dressing; grooming; food preparation; decision making; housekeeping; house maintenance; shopping; safety; meeting medical needs; security; communicating needs; administering medication; participating in activities with others; and orientation as to person, place, and time.

Mobility is the extent of movement within your environment. Consider your ability to go outside with or without help from another person and your ability to walk with or without assistance from devices such as a wheelchair or walker.

Eating refers here to your ability to get food, by any means, from the dish or glass into your body. Evaluate whether you can feed yourself with or without help from another person and any additional need to be fed by spoon, through a tube, or intravenously (IVs).

Bathing refers to getting to and from the bath, preparing bath water, toiletries, and handling equipment needed for washing your body. An important consideration is your ability to bathe with or without help from another person.

Dressing is the extent to which you can put on, fasten, and take off all items of your clothing.

Grooming is the extent you are able to handle such tasks as shampooing and combing your hair, brushing your teeth, and shaving. Your ability to dress and groom yourself with or without help from another person is an important consideration.

Food preparation is the extent to which you can cook and heat meals. Not only is your ability to prepare meals with or without help important, but the safety by which you prepare them must be considered.

Decision making has to do with your ability to make appropriate choices, to think clearly, and to make decisions without confusion.

Medication administration refers to the extent you are able to self-administer your daily medications as directed by your physician. You need to consider whether you take the prescribed dosage, choose the correct medication at the appropriate time, and reorder as needed.

Housekeeping is the extent to which you keep your house and clothes clean. Consider your ability to do housekeeping with or without help from another person and as often as it is needed.

House maintenance refers to your ability to maintain routine equipment, make house repairs, and do yard work. You need to consider whether you complete simple and major maintenance tasks with or without help from

another person as frequently as needed to preserve the value of your home.

Shopping is the extent you are able to get to the store, select groceries and other necessities, and get them home. Your ability to shop with or without help from another person, the number of shopping trips your needs require, and the available transportation are important considerations.

Safety refers to your ability to keep free from harm or injury by recognizing and remedying dangers such as exposed wiring, loose carpet or tile, and fire hazards.

Meeting medical needs assesses your health conditions that require special care, such as surgical dressing changes, oxygen, pressure breathing machines, incontinence care, tube feeding, suctioning, kidney dialysis, catheter/colostomy care, special skin care, physical therapy, occupational therapy, speech therapy, or other specialized medical procedures.

Security is the extent you are able (and remember) to lock your doors and windows. Some important considerations are whether you can secure locks on doors and windows with or without help from another person and if you feel secure within your living environment.

Communicating needs is your ability to make known to others, by any means, your specific needs and desires—a critically important consideration.

Participating in activities with others is the extent you are able to socialize and join in activities with others. Plan to consider your ability to get to and from activities and the dexterity to participate.

Orientation as to person, place, and time is the extent to which you are aware of who a person is; where you are; and what time, day, month, and year it is. Consider your ability to stay oriented with or without help from another person and how often you need help in such matters.

The following questions relate to the daily living activities just described. Answer them honestly. You'll discover your needs for assistance and be able to determine immediately whether you qualify for various housing and health care services. You will also be referred to later chapters that will assist you in making the right decision.

Daily Living Questions

Can you perform all activities required for daily living? _____
If your answer is yes, you qualify for independent living.
See Chapter 4.

Do you need assistance with getting dressed? _____
If your answer is yes, you may qualify for caregiving, assisted living, or residential care. See Chapters 3, 5, and 6.

Do you need assistance with meal preparation? _____
If your answer is yes, you may qualify for assisted living or residential care. See Chapters 5 and 6.

Do you need assistance with house and yard maintenance? _____
If your answer is yes, you may qualify for assisted living. See Chapter 5.

Do you need assistance with housekeeping? _____
If your answer is yes, you may qualify for assisted living. See Chapter 5.

Do you need assistance in daily bathing and grooming? _____
If your answer is yes, you may qualify for caregiving, assisted living, or residential care. See Chapters 3, 5, and 6.

Do you need assistance in administering and monitoring your daily medications? _____
If your answer is yes, you may qualify for caregiving, assisted living, or residential care. See Chapters 3, 5, and 6.

Do you need assistance with walking? _____
If your answer is yes, you may qualify for caregiving, assisted living, or residential care. See Chapters 3, 5, and 6.

Do you feel unsafe driving your automobile? _____
If your answer is yes, you may qualify for assisted living.
See Chapter 5.

Do you need assistance with grocery shopping? _____
If your answer is yes, you may qualify for assisted living.
See Chapter 5.

Do you need someone to go with you to the doctor's office? _____
If your answer is yes, you may qualify for assisted living.
See Chapter 5.

Do you need assistance in eating your meals? _____
If your answer is yes, you may qualify for caregiving, assisted living, or residential care. See Chapters 3, 5, and 6.

Have you lost control over bowels or bladder? _____
If your answer is yes, you may qualify for caregiving, nursing home care, or home health care. See Chapters 3, 8, and 15.

Do you require intravenous medications? _____
If your answer is yes, you may qualify for nursing home care or home health care. See Chapters 8 and 15.

Do you require periodic or continuous oxygen? _____
If your answer is yes, you may qualify for caregiving, assisted living, residential care, nursing home care, or home health care. See Chapters 3, 5, 6, 8, and 15.

Do you need treatment and care for pressure sores? _____
If your answer is yes, you may qualify for caregiving, nursing home care, or home health care. See Chapters 3, 8, and 15.

Do you need assistance to prevent you from falling? _____
If your answer is yes, you may qualify for caregiving or residential care. See Chapters 3 and 6.

Do you need care while you recover from an inpatient hospital stay? _____
If the answer is yes, you may qualify for caregiving, assisted living, residential care, nursing home care, or home health care. See Chapters 3, 5, 6, 8, and 15.

Do you need care to recover from an inpatient or outpatient surgical procedure? _____
If the answer is yes, you may qualify for caregiving, assisted living, residential care, nursing home care, or home health care. See Chapters 3, 5, 6, 8, and 15.

Once your basic strengths, abilities, and problems are identified, begin to match your needs with the services or resources available.

If the activities of daily living can be competently managed independently, your choices are to:

- Remain in your present home;

- Move to an apartment complex; or

- Move to a retirement center.

If the activities of daily living can be somewhat managed, but many activities require some assistance, or you discover that more specialized services are needed, your choices are to:

- Remain in your present home with the help of services such as transportation, home support, home-delivered meals, and other help;

- Move to an apartment complex with the help of support services as suggested above; or

- Move to a retirement center that provides on-site or contracted services designed to meet your needs.

If the activities of daily living cannot be managed in the majority of circumstances or in critical areas affecting your health and safety, your choices are to:

- Live in your home with support from a home care agency with private duty nursing and home support services;

- Live in a residential care setting with 24-hour supervision and assistance to meet your daily living needs; or

- Live in a nursing home setting that provides 24-hour nursing care and support services as directed by your doctor.

If the activities of daily living cannot be managed and if your health problems or disabilities requireconstant supervision by licensed professionals, your choice is to:

- Live in a nursing home setting that provides 24-hour nursing care and support services as directed by your doctor.

While each individual's situation varies, these guidelines and your honest evaluation of your ability to deal with the general activities of daily life are the starting points for your closer review of the referenced chapter or chapters. Each chapter will focus on a general understanding of the resources, services, and care available. You will be able to use further evaluation tools to assess your specific needs in order to make better decisions.

CHAPTER 2
SPEAKING THE LANGUAGE

The language used in the housing and health care industry is often confusing and frustrating if you do not have a general understanding of its terminology. Additionally, these terms and their usage vary from state to state and region to region. Therefore, this chapter provides a glossary of key terms for reference in understanding the content of this book and for greater ease in your investigation of housing and health care options.

Adult day care provides planned, supervised activities and meals in group settings for senior adults all or part of an entire day. These programs promote social, physical, and emotional well-being through personal attention and services. Some provide occupational, physical, or speech therapy with a physician's referral.

Adult foster care enables older adults to live with families or individuals who are willing to share their homes. Adult foster care offers these adults the option most like living in their own home.

Alzheimer's care usually is provided in a hospital or nursing home setting. Residents with Alzheimer's disease suffer with symptoms such as memory loss, disorientation, difficulty with words, poor judgment, dementia, and depression. Freedom of movement in a nonthreatening environment is essential. Therapeutic programs of care focus on persons' remaining abilities while minimizing their opportunities for failure.

Assisted living is similar to home support services but generally is provided within an apartment or patio home in a retirement center setting. The services provided enable senior adults to remain independent in their home rather than being placed in a higher level of care in the retirement center.

Caregiving is the care provided by another person or group of persons, usually within the home setting. This type of care can be given by the spouse, family members, or any person.

Catered living is another term for assisted living or home support and is usually provided in a retirement center setting. Occasionally, this term is used for residential care.

Congregate care is another term for independent living in a group setting such as a retirement center.

Continuing care retirement center (CCRC) is a retirement center that provides shelter, care, and services (including nursing home services) for as long as the resident lives in the facility in return for a one-time entrance fee and monthly fees.

Continuum of care is a term associated with a retirement center providing all levels of care for residents, such as independent living, assisted living, residential care, and nursing home care. As the residents' health status change, they can stay on the same campus without a change of address. The residents do not have to leave friends or staff with whom they feel comfortable.

Counseling services provide individuals and their families guidance and support in solving problems and making decisions.

Friendly visiting services provide regularly scheduled visits to the homebound or other isolated older adults for the purpose of offering companionship and expressing concern for their well-being.

Group home refers to a residential house that has been converted to accommodate several senior adults in a home setting and atmosphere. Staff can be specially trained or untrained, depending upon the group home and the needs of its residents.

Home delivered meal services offer nutritious meals to the homebound unable to prepare their own meals. Meals On Wheels is one well-known example of such services.

Home support is assistance provided within the home by external agencies or persons who manage such daily living tasks as housekeeping, laundry, limited maintenance, meal preparation, bathing, accompaniment to appointments, and shopping. It enables persons to maintain their independence in the quiet and convenience of their home with regular or intermittent personal attention. Generally, such services can be customized to fit any given situation.

Hospice care is a medical and supportive service for individuals who have been diagnosed with a terminal illness and have a life expectancy of six months or less. Its emphasis is supportive care rather than cure, comfort rather than rehabilitation.

Independent living is used primarily in conjunction with retirement centers. Typically, a person lives in an apartment or patio home within such a center. All the facilities, services, amenities, and freedoms of retirement living are available. Individuals can come and go as they please without having to depend upon the staff to provide the lifestyle they want to enjoy.

Intermediate care is the medium level of nursing home care, between personal care and skilled nursing care. Staff can provide more help than in personal care with such things as bathing, dressing, and getting in and out of bed or into a chair. Usually, more medical services are required also.

Occupational therapy is a medical service that promotes rehabilitation of social, recreational, and body mechanics needed for the routine activities of daily life. The goal is to increase persons' abilities to cope with daily life. Services are under the direction of a physician and are supervised by qualified occupational therapists.

Personal care is the lowest level of care provided within a nursing home. It is closely akin to residential care or supervisory care, however, certain types of care and assistance must be provided in a nursing home setting. For example, if residents cannot control bowels and bladder or if medications must be administered by licensed nursing personnel, these services must be provided under the supervision of licensed nursing staff. They cannot be performed by residential care staff.

Physical therapy is a medical service that promotes rehabilitation of the body through exercise and other types of stimulation. The goal is to increase physical abilities. Services are under the direction of a physician and are supervised by registered physical therapists.

Residential care is usually provided in a retirement center setting. This type of care provides an extra measure of assistance to persons who need 24-hour supervision. Aides insure that all residents receive three meals per day and daily monitoring of medications, and they supervise other activities of daily living as required. Housekeeping and laundry services are usually provided. There are private and semi-private rooms where residents can bring their own bed, furniture, and other personal belongings to make the room their home.

Respite care provides residential care usually for less than one month. This relieves individuals' families or friends of meeting continuous care needs for short periods of time. Some nursing homes and residential care homes offer this kind of care.

Self-care is managing the simple and complex activities of daily living and a certain limited amount of medical care for oneself.

Skilled care is the service provided in a nursing home setting by licensed nurses on a 24-hour basis.

Registered nurses—under the direction of a physician—supervise the care and/or the total assistance the staff provides to meet many or all of the residents' medical and physical needs.

Speech therapy is a medical service that promotes rehabilitation of speech. The goal is to increase speaking ability. Services are under the direction of a physician and are supervised by qualified speech therapists.

Sub-acute care is the highest level of medical care given in the nursing home setting. Usually, this type of care—rehabilitative services or continued medical and/or nursing care—is provided to residents after their discharge from the hospital. Medical care is under the direction of a physician, and daily care is supervised by registered nurses.

Supervisory care is another term for residential care.

Telephone reassurance provides a daily call to persons who live alone, who are anxious about safety or security, or those with health problems.

Transportation services offer rides to elderly or disabled persons who do not have private transportation or who are unable to use public transportation.

Summary

Spend time familiarizing yourself with these terms, particularly those multiple terms for the same type of service or care. You should refer frequently to this chapter as you seek to understand and make your retirement housing and health care decisions. Remember, a broad base of understanding is crucial in making sound decisions!

CHAPTER 3
CAREGIVING AT HOME

One of the greatest challenges facing the family today is providing proper care for aging parents. Grown children are now more likely to be responsible for their parents' care for a longer period of time than their parents invested in raising them. The average time of caregiving for aging parents is 18 years and rising.

Because parents are living longer, new and difficult situations occur in the lives of their median adult children. Among Christians comes the additional challenge to be obedient to God's command to honor father and mother. Does honoring your father and mother mean:

- Providing financial support for them?

- Changing careers to move closer to them?

- Having them live in your home?

- Quitting your job to become their caregiver?

- Loving them when they no longer recognize you?

- Passing up career advancement to give them more of your time?

These are hard questions that must be answered on a personal basis.

In this chapter, I will deal with the difficult subject of caregiving within the home. Caregiving can be defined as the provision of support and care to meet the activities of daily living of another person. This person could be your spouse, mother or father, grandparent, relative, or friend. Whatever the relationship, there are some practical aspects to caregiving that will be discussed in this chapter.

Caregiving by God's Plan

Many verses in God's Word offer guidance for those who are thinking of or are already providing care for others. Mark 7:9-13 records that the Pharisees used God as their excuse to avoid helping their families. They claimed it was more important to put money in the temple treasury than to help their needy parents, despite God's specific commands to honor fathers and mothers (see Ex. 20:12 and Eph. 6:2) and to care for those in need (see Lev. 25:35-43). You *should* give money and time to God, but we must never use God as an excuse to neglect our family or those in need we are able to help.

First Timothy 5:8 says, "But if any provide not for his own, and especially for those of his own house, he hath denied the faith, and is worse than an infidel." Those are harsh, strong words! Family relationships are important in God's eyes and an indicator of the vitality of our relationship to God.

The word *family* means all kinds of things to people today. Some view family from a traditional viewpoint: husband, wife, and children. Others view the family as a very loosely knit group of individuals without any formal roles, duties, or responsibilities.

In Ephesians 5 and 6, we find guidance for family members regarding roles within the Christian home. Ephesians 6:2 says, "Honor thy father and mother." How do we honor our father and mother? We honor them with our life, words, actions, lifestyle, vocation, and all we do. Everything about our lives ought to bring honor and demonstrate respect to our parents, no matter what age we or they are.

When Caregiving Is a Choice

Changes occur within the family that cause its adult members to seek alternatives to meet the specific needs of senior adults for personal support and care. Some changes resulting in such need are:

- Death of a spouse;

- Rehabilitation from surgery or physical illness;

- Change in health status;

- Loss of mobility;

- Personal safety concerns; and

- Ability to accomplish the tasks of daily living.

Unfortunately, many family members attempt to shift the biblical role and duties of the family for the care of its members to institutions to provide assistance, support, and care when it is unnecessary. Many senior adults could receive adequate care within the home if the potential caregivers knew about the variety of assistance available within most communities and how to access it.

The Young Approach

I asked Sue Young, Vice President of Marketing and Public Relations for Arizona Baptist Retirement Centers, to share the caregiving experience that she and her husband, Bill, are experiencing. I include their story to share the feelings, frustrations, and emotions that most caregivers have. You'll find comfort in knowing that others had reactions like yours when facing similar experiences.

Several years ago in February, my husband, Bill, and I were retiring for the night when we received a phone call that would change our lives.

Bill's parents lived in a small town about 90 miles away. His dad was almost completely confined to bed, suffering from Parkinson's disease and had recently been diagnosed as diabetic. Bill's mom was her husband's primary caregiver. In fact, she was the *only* caregiver because she would not allow anyone else to do much to help.

As I listened to Bill's side of the conversation, I realized something serious had happened to one of his parents. To our surprise, it was not Dad, but Mom, who had just been taken to the nearest hospital, leaving Dad in the care of neighbors until Bill could get there.

As we hurriedly prepared to leave, I learned that Mom had suffered a stroke, but had kept her composure and wits long enough to call 911 and the neighbors before collapsing to the floor.

Mom spent several days in the hospital in guarded condition, but finally recovered to the extent she was discharged to a rehabilitation hospital in Phoenix. The doctor told her she would no longer be able to care for Dad. We then made the only decision we could make, to take Dad home with us so that we could care for him.

After several days in the rehab center, Mom was discharged, having made a remarkable recovery from the stroke. She had to use a walker to keep her balance, but other than that, there were no visible signs that she had been ill. Still, we knew we would never feel secure about their well-being as long as they lived so far away. We decided to make the move a permanent one. We thus had three generations living in a four-bedroom house.

I'm not sure who has suffered the most through the three years since we made this change. Mom especially suffered from depression as she faced the fact that her independence and ability to do for herself were severely limited. She could no longer drive her car and run to the store when she felt like it. She was often bitter about the fact that so many of her prized possessions had to be sacrificed in order to combine our two households, but there simply was not enough room for all the "things" that had accumulated over the years.

She refused to take the medication the doctor prescribed for her depression, insisting that "everyone has bad days from time to time." Bill suddenly had to change his routine and plan his day around the needs of both parents. Fortunately, he owned his own business and was able to set his own hours, but he spent many days just taking care of the two of them.

I had to adjust to the reality of my mother-in-law, to whom I had never felt particularly close, moving in and taking over my kitchen, my home, and, sometimes it seemed, my whole life.

Our college-aged daughter, who was living at home at the time, grew impatient with what she considered "Grandma's snooping" in her business and the endless questioning of where she was going, when she was returning, and who she was seeing. She eventually began to avoid her grandmother as much as possible.

Mom gradually improved to the point that she insisted on taking over the role as Dad's caregiver once again. While we argued with her and tried to convince her that was not in her best interest, we were up against the same resolve and determination that had brought her through the stroke, seemingly unscathed.

Since then, Dad's health has continued to decline. Mom has had several surgeries and health problems herself. We moved to a bigger home so everyone could have more privacy; soon after, our daughter became engaged and was married over a year ago.

Mom still gives Dad all of her time, even though she now allows a home health agency to provide some minor care three days a week. Bill has had to take a more active role in caring for his dad, which means he sometimes has to get up several times a night or reschedule his plans during the day. We have discussed the possibility of eventually placing Dad in a nursing home, but we know Mom will never allow it as long as she is able to keep going.

Unfortunately, Mom will not be able to keep this up. It has been extremely frustrating to my family to see how she insists on sacrificing her own health to care for Dad. In the end, everyone loses, but until another crisis develops, this is the way she wants it.

We still have our differences, and there are days when we get on each other's nerves; but for the most part, we have all made adjustments and learned to live in harmony with one another. It's all a part of being family.

Sue and Bill's experiences are duplicated all over the United States every day. Families are affected by the necessary caregiving for an older adult within the home. I hope this chapter provides some measure of guidance and assistance in understanding practical steps you must take to effectively provide caregiving within your home.

I also realize that certain circumstances family members face do not allow them to care for parents or other relatives at home. Some of these include geographical and/or financial limitations, two-career families, physical incapacity, health status, and other work responsibilities. However, it is my belief that senior adults do much better in a home setting if there is appropriate assistance and help.

Many middle-aged adults are caught between caring for their elderly parents and their own children. They are called "the sandwich generation." Living happily in an extended family calls for maximum patience, love, understanding, and wisdom on the part of all persons involved.

Whether you continue living at home will depend on your own health problems, disabilities, and whether there are supportive services close to home and individuals who can provide caregiving functions.

Caregiving can be implemented best by understanding the following four important elements:

- Identification of caregiving needs;

- External resources for caregiving assistance;

- Specialized services and resources; and

- Understanding and recognizing when caregiving is insufficient.

1. Identification of caregiving needs

Identifying caregiving needs can best be accomplished by using the daily living questions in Chapter 1. Once your basic strengths, abilities, and problems are identified, you should begin to match your needs with available services or resources mentioned later in this chapter.

2. External resources for caregiving assistance

Family and friends are two of the best resources for caregiving assistance. But there are other supportive services in most communities. With the exception of adult foster care, support groups, and group dining, the supportive services described below are designed to come to your home, as are the services provided by home health agencies.

Support services do not require state licensure to open for business. However, many of them are licensed or certified by city or county governments. The following list includes common resources for caregiving assistance at home. You'll recognize many of these terms from the glossary in Chapter 2.

Adult foster care enables older adults to live with families or with individuals willing to share their homes. Adult foster care offers the arrangement most similar to living in your own home.

Support groups can meet a variety of specialized needs such as coping with the personal toll of caregiving, Alzheimer's disease, grief and bereavement, loss, and other needs.

Group dining offers a nutritious noon meal and social activities to older persons at places such as senior adult centers, churches, or schools. Often, transportation is available to those sites.

Adult protective services will provide legal and financial counseling to people unable to manage their own affairs or to protect themselves. These services are designed to prevent or remedy the neglect and abuse of adults.

Chore maintenance provides heavy indoor cleaning and may include designated outdoor tasks.

Counseling services give individuals and their families guidance and support to solve problems. Many agencies offer individualized and customized counseling services.

Friendly visiting services provide regular, scheduled visits to the homebound or isolated persons, offering companionship and concern for these persons' well-being.

Home-delivered meal services bring nutritious meals to the homebound unable to cook their own meals.

Household work services provide assistance with routine household maintenance for persons who cannot do these activities.

Shopping services provide grocery shopping for persons homebound due to illness/medical limitations.

Telephone reassurance provides a daily call to persons who live alone, who are anxious about safety or security, and to persons who have health problems.

Transportation services offer rides to elderly or disabled persons who do not have private transportation or who are unable to use public transportation.

3. Specialized services and resources

Respite care provides residential care for an individual for short periods of time, usually for less than one month. This temporarily relieves family and friends from continuous care responsibilities. Some nursing care institutions and residential care homes provide this kind of care.

Caregivers who understand they need a rest and some personal time will become more effective caregivers and probably be able to continue caregiving for a longer period of time. When persons go without help or a break from constant caregiving duties, they are attempting an impossible mission and will be setting themselves up for eventual breakdown.

Constantly caring for another person takes its toll in stress and fatigue, affecting the health and overall well-being of the care provider. Studies indicate that lack of respite care may be the number one factor leading to a premature nursing home placement of older adults.

The earlier respite care is introduced into the caregiving setting, the better for all concerned. Respite care is especially effective when it is scheduled regularly. The individual receiving the caregiving may also benefit from respite by having someone different to interact with at home or outside the home.

Many community organizations and services offer respite care to caregivers. These volunteer organizations and long-term care providers offer safe respite opportunities for short or extended periods of time in:

- The caregiver's home;

- Adult day care centers;

- Residential care facilities; or

- Nursing homes.

Fees can be expensive; however, costs vary according to the type of service and the agency. Sliding scale fees or scholarships may be available. Others occasionally offer free services through coupons. Some in-home care agencies use volunteers and are free. Families may qualify for financial assistance through various agencies such as the Department of Economic Security, Medicaid, and the Veterans Administration.

Adult day care provides planned, supervised activities and meals in a group setting for all or part of an entire day. Day care services promote social, physical, and emotional well-being through personal attention and meeting individual needs. Some day care centers provide physical, speech, and occupational therapy services with a physician's referral.

Adult day care centers providing supervision in a group setting for elderly and disabled people who live at home have multiplied tenfold in the past decade to over 3,000 nationally. This trend will only accelerate since the number of frail parents per adult child will nearly double by the year 2030, and families will provide 80 percent of needed long-term care.

Adult day care centers are intended for those individuals who cannot function independently or as a placement for individuals receiving caregiving. Typically, adult day care centers provide:

- Supervision during daytime hours;

- Therapeutic recreational programs;

- Personal care and hygiene facilities;

- Snacks and hot noon meals;

- Transportation;

- Health maintenance, screening, and monitoring;

- Socialization, companionship, and new friendships;

- Social work services such as counseling or support groups; and

- Respite for caregivers.

Adult day care centers understand the necessity for caregivers to have free time and encourage caregivers to take care of their personal business, get uninterrupted rest, attend caregiver support groups, or just take a break.

The odds are good that somebody in your family will need adult day care. Adult day care centers are not alike; each will offer varied services. Centers range from homes and churches to new medical buildings with nurses and physical therapy available. The programs planned range from day-long television watching to theme weeks with drama groups and field trips. Many centers also offer transportation, physical therapy, occupational therapy, speech therapy, caregiving support groups, and other services.

Adult day care centers can delay nursing home placement by an average of 15-22 months according to some studies. Costs range from $20 to $50 per day, and these facilities can serve nearly anyone who is not bedridden.

Several special aspects to look for when choosing an adult day care center are as follows:

- Written policies on fees and emergency procedures;

- A written, up-to-date plan of care for each participant;

- Planned menus and meals for those on special diets;

- A plan for daily communication with caregivers;

- Referrals to other needed services;

- Active, involved staff trained in CPR and first aid;

- A warm, inviting atmosphere;

- Adequate space, furniture, and equipment, both indoors and outdoors; and

- A variety of appealing activities.

The setting should be safe and clean with at least one trained staff person for every six adults. The staff should be trained to recognize medical problems and to respond to medical emergencies.

A center should offer clients opportunities to interact through activities that are age-appropriate and reflect clients' life experiences and interests. Normally, activities are planned on a monthly basis, and the facility should post its activity calendar for each month.

Families who need financial assistance should ask center personnel about private grants or state aid programs accepted at these day care centers. Medicaid can be used for adult day care in about 35 states. A growing number of private, long-term care insurance policies also now cover adult day care.

Home health care provides medical services as ordered by a physician in the home of homebound patients. Services and visits include licensed nurses, nursing assistants, medical social services, physical therapy, occupational therapy, speech therapy, and respiratory therapy.

The importance of home health care cannot be overemphasized in making caregiving at the home a more workable option. Chapter 15 details this medical service.

Hospice care provides support for terminally ill patients and their families. Its emphasis is supportive care rather than curative, comfort rather than rehabilitation. Because of its importance, Chapter 16 explains this medical service.

4. Understanding and recognizing when caregiving is insufficient

Whether caregiving continues in the home setting should be determined by several key factors. Usually, it is determined by the helplessness of the individual receiving caregiving services or by physical needs exceeding the level of training or expertise of the caregiver. Additionally, the ability of the caregiver to continue to provide the necessary care is a strong determining factor. Often families lose their caregiver, and others in the family cannot perform caregiving functions.

When you need continuous health care for an extended period of time, a nursing home may be the best or only answer. The choice of such a home-away-from-home becomes appropriate when the need is particularly great and community options are not adequate or available.

Often the family and the physician make the decision to seek nursing home care. As much as possible, it is important to involve the older adult in the decision-making process, too. When older people are unable to participate in the decision to move into a nursing home, their family members may feel overwhelmed with guilt or despair over their decision. But when nursing home care truly is the best option for the older person, loved ones can feel great comfort in making the right choice.

At such times, plan to seek outside counsel from the senior adult's physician and other medical advisors. Often a geriatric assessment is beneficial, and these can be performed by many acute care hospitals and other diagnostic centers. Home health care agencies offer geriatric assessments as well.

Evaluating Your Ability to Provide Caregiving at Home

If questions do not apply, pass over them. Otherwise, check the appropriate response for each question.

1. Does the home or apartment have an extra room with easy access to a bathroom?
____ yes (0)   ____ no (1)

2. Can you afford the additional expense of providing care not covered by insurance?
____ yes (0)   ____ no (1)

3. Will a responsible adult be available to watch the patient at home?
____ yes (0)   ____ no (1)

4. Do all adults in the family have to work outside the home?
____ yes (0)   ____ no (1)

If the answer is yes, will there be a responsible family member available to supervise care at home?
____ yes (0)   ____ no (1)

5. Is there someone to relieve the primary caregiver within the family?
____ yes (0)   ____ no (1)

6. Are there young children at home who require supervision?
____ yes (1)   ____ no (0)

7. Are there teenagers at home?
____ yes (1)   ____ no (0)

If the answer to 7. is yes, evaluate their reaction to adjusting such activities as when and how often friends visit, how loudly music is played, and expectations for their relationship with the older adult(s) involved.

Do you anticipate problems?
____ I do not anticipate problems in adjusting. (0)
____ I foresee conflict over one or more such issues. (1)

8. Do you have the emotional stability to deal with elderly or sick people?
____ yes (0)   ____ no (1)

9. Do you fear the aging process for yourself?
____ yes (2)   ____ not sure (1)
____ no (0)

10. Did you have a difficult time growing up when dealing with your mother or father?
____ yes (1)   ____ no (0)

If the answer is yes, were these difficult issues ever resolved?
____ yes (0)   ____ no (1)

11. Is there a basic personality clash between you and your parent?
____ yes (1)   ____ no (0)

12. Evaluate your feelings about providing care for your parent.
____ very uncomfortable (4)
____ somewhat uncomfortable (3)
____ not sure (2)
____ able to accept the changes (1)
____ very comfortable (0)

13. Imagine your reactions if you had to feed your parents or change their diapers.

_____ could never do this (4)
_____ don't think I could do it (3)
_____ not sure (2)
_____ would not bother me (1)
_____ comfortable (0)

14. Will the patient require a variety of rehabilitation programs such as physical therapy, occupational therapy, or speech therapy?

_____ yes (1)   _____ no (0)

If the answer is yes, are these programs available through home health care services?

_____ yes (1)   _____ no (0)

15. Is home health care available in your community?

_____ yes (0)   _____ no (1)

If the answer is yes, are there long waiting lists or limitations on the type and extent of care provided?

_____ yes (1)   _____ no (0)

16. Has the patient always been a social individual?

_____ yes (0)   _____ no (1)

If the answer is yes, are there options for a variety of social activities at home?

_____ yes (0)   _____ no (1)

Now, add up the point value of each answer to determine your total score.

My total score: _____

- If your score is 10 or under, you are a good candidate for providing caregiving in the home.

- If you scored 11 to 20, your ability to handle caregiving at the home is questionable.

- If you scored 21 or over, you should definitely explore an external caregiver or nursing home care for your elderly relative.

Coping with Negative Feelings

If you are the caregiver, please realize there will be negative feelings toward yourself and toward the individual for whom you are caring. These are natural reactions, but many times caregivers do not recognize they've developed negative feelings or are embarrassed to admit they exist. Both reactions are unhealthy.

Accept assistance from others to deal with your negative feelings and to express any hostile feelings. If you are the caregiver, try to recognize and acknowledge these negative feelings. Many caregivers are ashamed or fearful of such honesty. At the same time, when negative, hostile feelings are dealt with as they occur, you will rediscover the joy of caregiving. It is an experience that you will never forget and will look back on with great satisfaction.

Explore alternatives for coping

with your negative feelings by joining a support group for caregivers or sharing your feelings with a favorite minister or a trusted friend. Look for the community services and other resources mentioned in this chapter that can help you to provide the necessary care.

Summary

Caregiving is only an option with the availability of someone to provide it. Obviously, the best caregiver is a close family member, relative, or friend. Senior adults simply do better and feel more secure when they are in familiar places with familiar people. However, when this is not possible, use the following guidelines in choosing an unfamiliar caregiver:

- Contact personal references. Ask them to evaluate whether the applicant is a loving and caring person.

- Check for previous experience with senior adults, such as in residential care or nursing home care.

- Consider physical abilities and any physical limitations.

- Insist that any caregiver has training in CPR and other medical emergencies.

- Evaluate the person's language and communication skills as

compatible with the one to receive caregiving.

- Require documentation of a "clean bill of health."

Before you make your final decision and actually choose an external caregiver, attend to these final details:

- Make sure the caregiver has been given specific and written instructions about your expectations. Provide a daily routine list.

- Have an attorney prepare a "Caregiver Agreement" to be signed by both parties, witnessed, and notarized. It should list all conditions of employment such as duties, specific hours, and wages.

- Under no circumstances should the name of the caregiver be placed on checking accounts, savings accounts, or any other document without consulting an attorney.

- The caregiver should not handle money if it can be avoided.

- Never grant a durable power of attorney to the caregiver.

- Never make a caregiver the beneficiary of any will or trust.

The caregiver's role is so important because he or she is

taking care of your parent, relative, or friend. Experience, along with many sad stories, has led me to conclude that all the details mentioned above are vital. A properly prepared agreement, even with members of your own family, will save you a great deal of grief, heartache, and financial abuse. It will be well worth the effort and expense. Remember, only *you* have the right and ability to keep yourself from being abused.

Exhibit 1 is a bibliography entitled "The Family and Caregiving for the Elderly." These references will be helpful to you in dealing with caregiving options and decisions within the home.

I am a strong advocate of caregiving at home if at all possible. I believe it is a family responsibility and an obligation from a biblical perspective. However, I also realize circumstances can prevent family members from performing the caregiving themselves. Do not feel guilty over this circumstance if it happens in your family. The most important consideration is to meet the affected senior adult's personal and medical needs. This can be accomplished by choosing an appropriate caregiver and by utilizing the vast resources available in your community.

Personal Planning

The following two pages are the first of several throughout the book that provide space for you to make personal plans based on what you have read. I encourage you to use these pages to highlight steps you need to complete later, or to make a list of ideas you will want to consider in more detail.

Personal Planning

Personal Planning

SECTION 2
RETIREMENT HOUSING OPTIONS

CHAPTER 4

INDEPENDENT LIVING

As a person's years advance, moving—or even the idea of moving—seems to create a great many fears. In life's later years, familiar surroundings, family, and old friends feel more comfortable and secure because they are the biggest part of anyone's life. Whether people or possessions, they are beloved, and it is normal to want to enjoy them in the years ahead.

Sooner or later, you may find that your living arrangements are no longer a good match with your physical needs and capabilities. Your dwelling may be too big, too hard to keep up, or require too many repairs. Then, even though you like living in your home, you are free to consider moving to some other community once your job no longer dictates where you must live.

Many older people will face housing decisions; fortunately, in most communities more solutions are available now than ever before for senior adult housing.

For senior adults contemplating the advantages and disadvantages of relocating, a variety of retirement housing options exist. However, you need to ask yourself these important questions before you make your final decision:

- What are the initial and ongoing costs required by this new housing?

- In what kind of community am I wanting to live?

- What type of climate is most suitable for me?

- How much isolation and/or freedom do I want?

- Do I want to move where my neighbors or other residents are much like me?

- What physical capacities and/or limitations do I have?

- How close is the proposed housing area to my family and friends?

- Does the cost of living limit where I live?

- If I have health problems, how accessible will a hospital, nursing home, physicians, and other medical services be to me?

- How close are recreational activities that I enjoy?

These valid questions must be answered prior to your seeking alternative housing.

Careful advance planning also must consider your personal needs, desires, and resources, not only for the immediate future, but as you envision they may be in a decade or two. It is always wise, if not essential, to visit an area before settling there and to make careful inspection of the housing in which you wish to reside before you make any financial or legal commitments.

Deciding about new living arrangements can be compared to making any other major purchase. You need to look to see if it meets your basic requirements. Trust your initial judgment. Finally, you have to decide if you can afford it.

To begin this process, obtain a list of the various types of senior adult housing in your area. Start with your local Area Agency on Aging, social services agency, senior center, your doctor, civic or religious organizations, or browsing the yellow pages. Another good resource to contact is anyone you personally know who has made such a housing decision recently.

Try to plan ahead. Make visits, ask questions, and discuss alternatives with your friends and family. Look below the surface, ask for references, and make inquiries. Get a clear picture of all the costs, and be sure you uncover all hidden charges. Always keep your financial situation in mind. Do not hesitate to ask the hard questions. Remember, you are making an important decision requiring a significant investment, and you will want to get all the facts first.

You may find a range of prices for the same type of housing arrangement. Be sure you understand what you are getting when you choose a particular type of housing. Start by making a list of the sites in your area you want to visit.

Reasons to Stay in Your Present Home

Start your analysis of your options for retirement housing by determining whether your own home is still an option. The following list offers some reasons to stay in your present home. Read each statement and then circle either true or false, whichever is the right answer for you.

- My home fits my individual needs.
  True   False

- My family and friends live nearby.
  True   False

- I am near shopping centers, my church, and recreational centers.
  True   False

- This neighborhood meets my individual needs for social and cultural activities.
  True   False

- This neighborhood is well-maintained, and I feel secure in this location.
  True   False

- My doctor, needed medical facilities, and other professional services are nearby.
  True   False

- The expenses of my home are not a strain on my budget.
  True   False

If you marked most or all statements true for you, then you have argued effectively to continue to live in your present home.

Possible Reasons to Relocate

There are also good reasons to consider relocating to another kind of retirement housing. Carefully read the reasons below and circle either true or false, whichever is the right answer for you.

- My home is difficult and/or too expensive to maintain.
  True   False

- It is becoming more difficult for me to do regular household chores.
  True   False

- Too much of my money is tied up in my home equity; I need to sell this house to provide additional income to meet my daily needs.
  True   False

- My health status is declining to the extent that I need help with daily living.
  True   False

- It is increasingly difficult for me to get to shopping centers, doctors, dentists, church, and recreational facilities.
  True   False

- My neighborhood is not as nice nor as safe as it once was.
  True   False

If you marked most or all statements true for you, then you have found compelling reasons to consider relocating. You will most likely be choosing one of the housing options that follow.

Types of Retirement Housing

Many of these retirement housing options are available throughout the United States. Your choice from among them will depend on many different factors and your particular needs. The following summary of the major options in retirement housing will help you begin to make this choice.

1. *Condominium living* is housing in an apartment building or townhouse. Couples or individuals hold title to their living unit, but share the common areas with other owners in the development. In addition, monthly condominium fees are collected to maintain this common property. Additionally, the managing board may make special assessments to acquire reserve funds for major expenditures that will occur during the life of the development.

2. *Echo housing* is a self-contained, freestanding, removable living unit occupied by a relative on the same property and adjacent to a single family home. It permits closeness to family without sacrificing personal self-reliance. You should contact your local zoning office to determine whether echo units are legal in your area.

3. *Shared housing* is another new option being explored by individuals, communities, and the government as a way to provide adequate, affordable housing for older people.

Shared housing involves several persons—usually unrelated—living together, with private space for individuals and shared common areas such as bath or kitchen for all residents. It combines the benefits of living in a house with the need to share expenses and chores.

House sharing may involve joining an existing group set up in a private house or in a house owned by a public or private agency, or it may involve renting out an extra bedroom in your own home. House sharing is not for everyone. Explore and negotiate a workable arrangement before making a commitment.

4. *Low income housing* complexes often reserve some of their public housing units for the elderly who have low incomes. The need for more low and moderate cost housing for the elderly is well recognized. Two federal agencies are responsible for helping states and communities expand this housing option to more of the senior adults who qualify for it. The Department of Housing and Urban Development (HUD) is the agency principally involved in providing low income housing units where rent is set according to a sliding scale schedule for each resident. HUD housing is usually offered in an apartment or high-rise building designed for groups of individuals.

The Farmers Home Administration oversees a program of federal aid for constructing houses, including rental houses, for older people in rural areas.

5. *Mobile manufactured homes* are increasingly attractive to older adults as a housing option. Not only are they attracted to the mobile home communities designed for a senior adult population, but

affordability, space, and energy efficiency make them desirable.

6. *Retirement communities* are self-contained complexes that provide housing and at least minimal services to their residents. Some retirement communities are also continuing care centers where houses, apartments, and nursing homes, along with other needed services, are all available.

For purposes of this book and in the bulk of this chapter, I focus primarily on the option of a retirement community for independent living. Its level of housing affords independence for the resident while also including a variety of services to meet the needs of residents' lifestyles.

Professional Builder magazine, in its September 1985 issue, stated:

Retirement housing is more than simply housing in which elderly people live. While it may take on many physical attributes of family housing, such as high-rise construction, planned communities of single family residences, or campus-type environments of multi-unit, low-rise dwellings with common use recreation centers, elderly housing in addition caters to the particular physical and emotional needs and desires of its clientele.

Independent living is an ideal option for the carefree retirement many senior adults have always

envisioned. Residents can come and go as they please while they enjoy life to the fullest. Most retirement housing campuses offer a variety of activities and recreational opportunities to accommodate the most active lifestyle.

An independent living decision, often made by a couple, widow, or adult children for their parent, generally is regarded as the last move ever to be made. The transit to other levels of care and meeting future needs may become issues in the future, but they will not have the impact of the first move to a retirement community.

Five categories of information need to be gathered in order to finalize any decision for housing in a retirement community. These are:

1. Price or costs;

2. Security;

3. Meeting needs (levels of care, amenities);

4. Learning about the interests and backgrounds of other residents; and

5. Location (close to family, friends, or doctors).

These categories provide the boundaries within which people decide about moving to a retirement community and how they gather the information about the community. This process begins to alleviate their fears, doubts, anxieties, and concerns about this important decision coming so late in life.

One of the most common errors made by senior adults in deciding whether to move to a retirement housing complex is delaying the decision until their options are limited or their failing health dictates a specific decision. Often that decision is made at an emotional time in their lives. Therefore, the final decision is not made objectively and results in some poor choices.

My suggestion is to start early in your retirement years to explore your housing options. The most common statement I hear is, "I will move to a retirement center later, but I do not feel old enough now!" The fact is, such a move should be contemplated early in retirement age while various options still can be considered in an objective manner.

You might be surprised how early in life many people start looking for a retirement center. Their decision-making process often takes six months to two years to complete. Most senior adults tend to make housing decisions slowly. Not only are they choosing the destination of their last move, but they will be adjusting to less living space and disposing of cherished furniture and other belongings. Of utmost importance is living an individually chosen lifestyle and maintaining the highest level of independence possible for them at all times.

Criteria for Independent Living

Independent living is designed specifically for active, independent retirees who wish to enjoy their senior years in a flourishing retirement community. Residents in the community have complete freedom to come and go as they please, assured that their residence is maintained by professional staff. The chart on the next page details some criteria frequently used by potential residents evaluating a retirement center.

Residents cannot rely on neighbors or staff to assist in these functional areas. Sometimes a short-term need arises and is met by a staff member or neighbor in a controlled manner as assessed by the staff.

Physical Design of Housing Units

Retirement housing complexes usually offer a variety of physical designs for apartments or residential homes. Generally, there are studio or efficiency apartments and one- and two-bedroom apartments. Then occasionally, retirement centers offer larger garden apartments or residential homes that allow more square feet of living space.

Units should be designed to accommodate residents when they are independent and later when they may need personal assistance. Certain design features are

Functional Area	Functional Level
Mobility	Independently mobile with or without assistive devices, or has wheelchair mobility, including transfer in and out of chair.
Bowels and bladder	Continent or personally responsible for own care of indwelling catheter, colostomy, or disposable briefs.
Medications	All are taken independently, without help or assistance.
Treatments	All are managed independently without help or assistance.
Social Skills	Able to communicate effectively and appropriately. Occasionally may have slight confusion or memory lapse. Initiates self-care.
Necessary daily tasks	All are accomplished independently without help or assistance.

important—skid-proof floors, lowered switches and elevated outlets that do not require residents to reach or crouch, grab bars at bathtubs and toilets, doors wide enough for wheelchairs, emergency call buttons, and similar conveniences. In addition, living units that are at ground level or accessible by elevator generally are preferable to those reached only by stairs.

Other design considerations may also include special soundproofing measures, extra non-glare lighting, avoiding certain colors, automatic doors, certain corridor dimensions, specially positioned sinks and mirrors, careful furniture selections, and numerous other factors related to the visual, auditory, or ambulatory impairments that may accompany older age.

Choosing between one-story or multi-story facilities is difficult. There are advantages to both. One-story apartments offer convenient entry, close parking spaces, and seem to suit handicapped residents better. Multi-story facilities offer better views of the surrounding area, closeness to other residents, and the appearance of improved security. Most seniors living in our retirement centers want one-story apartments. However, it is a matter of personal preference and determined by specific needs.

The elderly tend to prefer the larger units over the smaller units, probably because they move from their larger homes into a smaller apartment. It is difficult to dispose of furniture, household items, keepsakes, and other property.

The affluent elderly occupy a small percentage of retirement housing. Facilities designed to attract them offer luxurious two- and three-bedroom apartments, usually with 2,000 to 2,500 square feet of living space, and loaded with recreational amenities in the complex. However, the majority of retirement housing occupants are middle income people. Most of these senior adults want the following interior design in their house or apartment.

1. Privacy within the living unit is essential, especially to older couples. Even common areas, both indoors and outdoors, ought to provide some measure of privacy while maximizing the opportunity for residents to meet face-to-face. This may explain why efficiency or studio apartments are far less popular than one- or two-bedroom apartments.

2. Feeling secure inside and outside the living unit is a must. Most every retirement housing community has security doors with alarm systems and emergency call systems monitored 24 hours a day. Many also put security guards at various key spots in the complex.

3. Liberal use of natural light in individual living units and all common areas is important. All corridors, lobbies, and apartments should offer views to the outside. Careful attention also should be given to artificial light levels. As people age, they need access to more light.

4. Because they perceive heat and cold very differently, senior adults need individually controlled heating and cooling.

5. Large areas of unbroken wall space make furniture placement easy. An open space plan that allows ease of movement—with or without a wheelchair—is usually good. Small, walled-in areas should be avoided.

6. Careful attention should be given to barriers such as high doorsteps, multiple living levels, uneven walking surfaces, thick carpet (which is hard for older persons to walk on), hard to open doors (lever handles overcome this barrier), and plumbing fixtures that require strength and dexterity to operate.

7. Look for other safety features not immediately apparent, such as large bathrooms, seats in all showers, non-slip floors, and wide doors. Electrical outlets and plugs should be accessible without bending or reaching.

8. Storage space is critical. It is almost impossible to provide too much closet or display space. The elderly have many prized items. Built-in bookcases are popular.

9. Flexibility in adjusting shelving, closet rods, and even bath and kitchen counter heights is an important feature.

10. Kitchens are a powerful drawing card. The most popular choice is a compact kitchen with at least 30 inches of counter space, useable while seated, with unobstructed views of the dining and living room area. Dishwashers are not a must because many senior adults have few dishes to wash. Top-mounted freezers should be avoided. All appliances need front-mounted, easy-to-read dials and gauges.

11. Laundry facilities should be located in each apartment or at least on the main living level, not in a basement.

12. Mail delivery areas should have easy access. Large graphics on housing units and mailboxes enable residents to identify their units and mailboxes or slots easily.

13. Elevators must be large enough for wheelchairs and with doors that close slowly to avoid possible injury.

14. The bathroom design is important. Most older people want only one bathroom; however, the affluent elderly usually want at least two. Separating the toilet area from the tub and shower is desirable. Bathrooms should have wide doors and be large enough to allow a wheelchair to maneuver in them. There should be a dressing table with a sink that a seated person can easily use. Showers are more popular than bathtubs.

15. Entry doors should have peepholes at two levels, the lower accessible to a seated person. All entries should be well lighted.

16. Bedrooms ought to be large enough for a wheelchair to move around the bed. One-bedroom units are the most popular while efficiency or studio apartments are the least popular. When judging the overall desirability of a facility, do not be taken in by the scope of the outdoor common areas. The best designed common areas will not make up for a lack of adequate size or privacy in the living units themselves.

Convenience Services

Services are what distinguish retirement housing most from any other form of housing. Services offered by many retirement communities may be likened to those provided in the hotel or hospitality industries. They may include restaurants or group dining facilities, weekly or periodic housekeeping and flat laundry services, game rooms, fitness centers, tennis, golf, pool and spa facilities, barber shops and beauty salons, on-site banks, convenience stores and gift shops, local minibus transportation, arts and crafts areas, and a host of other programs and features often designed by an activities director. In addition to the quality of the physical surroundings, the extent and scope of these services will differentiate luxury facilities from those directed to the lower and middle income population. Luxury retirement facilities are modeled after a resort lifestyle.

In my experience, surveys indicate that food service, social programs and activities, common meeting rooms, housekeeping, laundry, and transportation rank as the highest priorities.

Quality of Life Amenities

Probably one of the most important considerations in choosing between retirement housing options is the available amenities to enhance the quality of life for residents. The three most important are 1) meal services, 2) recreational choices, and 3) the availability of additional necessary services.

Meal services are important because nutritional concerns are especially critical with age. Most independent living facilities offer group dining at least one meal a day. Larger facilities will offer three meals a day in a cafeteria-style dining room. Waitresses are often available to assist residents with individual needs. Often, at least one meal is included with the fee schedules. Optional meal plans afford residents a variety of menus to meet their individual diet requirements for health problems.

Recreational services vary with retirement centers. Many offer pools, spas, shuffleboard, miniature golf, putting greens, and crafts and woodworking shops—to mention a few. Recreation is important for senior adults to retain their dexterity and good health. It also affords social interaction with other residents. Most centers post activity calendars; studying these will help in the evaluation and decision-making process.

The availability of necessary services is probably the *most important* consideration in the decision-making process. As a resident's health status changes, available services become increasingly important for staying in the apartment setting. Some of the more important services are housekeeping, laundry, assistance with bathing and dressing, meal preparation, and transportation.

Entrance Requirements and Agreements

While entrance requirements for retirement centers offering independent living vary by ownership, there are basically four models. These are 1) lease agreements, 2) buy-in agreements, 3) life tenancy agreements, and 4) life care agreements.

The one used most often is the lease agreement. However, many owners offer multiple plans to fit the prospective resident's desires or particular needs.

The *lease agreement* is a simple basic rental plan. The agreement usually requires a deposit of a few hundred dollars, the first month's rent in advance, and the signing of an initial 12-month lease document. After the initial lease period, the agreement extends on a month-to-month basis.

Exhibit 2 is a sample of a typical lease agreement used in a retirement center offering independent living.

The advantage of the lease agreement is that the payment is modest and any additional income and savings can be invested in an interest-bearing account.

The *buy-in agreement* is based on an established sales price for the apartment determined by two components: 1) resident equity, and 2) entrance endowment. The resident does not buy the apartment, but rather the right to live in the apartment as long as health allows

Resident equity is the portion of the sales price the resident always retains. While this amount usually does not earn interest, it is available to the resident upon discharge or to the estate in case of death.

Entrance endowment is the portion of the sales price usually earned by the owner over a three-year period (1/36 each month of residency). The unearned portion of entrance endowment is refunded if discharge occurs during the first three years of residency.

The split between resident equity and entrance endowment is based on a table reflecting the age of the resident or, in case of a couple, the younger spouse.

Exhibit 3 is a sample of a typical buy-in agreement utilized in a retirement center setting for independent living.

In the sample buy-in agreement, you can see that the 50/50 split of resident equity and entrance endowment is at 70 years of age. This split varies by owner. However, the older a resident is at admission, the larger amount of resident equity.

Let's assume the prospective resident, Carl, is 70 years of age, and the sales price of his apartment is $60,000. Upon his admission, Carl would pay $60,000 to the owner. Carl's equity would be $30,000, which is always available at discharge, and entrance endowment would be $30,000. The owner would earn 1/36th of $30,000 each month for 36 months. If Carl lives in the apartment a full three years, he will not be eligible to receive any portion of the original entrance endowment. However, if he lives in the apartment for only one year, two years' worth of entrance endowment would be refunded along with the full amount of his equity.

Typically, if the center is constructing a new apartment, the center will require one-third of the sales price upon execution of the agreement, one-third of the sales price when the walls and roof are in place, and the final one-third upon the receipt of a certificate of occupancy.

The *life tenancy agreement* is based upon the life expectancy of the resident at the time of entrance. It is developed using tables that establish the value of the dollar over a period of time, using life expectancy as a determinant.

Life tenancy agreements require an up-front purchase fee with monthly service charges to offset the direct operational costs of the center. Residents actually prepay the rent in one lump sum entrance fee and have the right to live in the apartment for their entire lives. Residents can sublease the unit if they stop living on the premises. The income from any sublease belongs to the original resident. Usually, life tenancy agreements are irrevocable and no refunds are given at the time of discharge.

Exhibit 4 is a sample of a typical life tenancy agreement used in a retirement center including independent living.

The *life care agreement* is usually available in continuing care retirement centers with multiple levels of care. Basically, life care agreements require a large lump sum entrance fee that pays for taking care of the resident for life, regardless of the actual cost of such care. A monthly service fee is required on a continuing basis. As health status changes, the resident moves into other levels of care, but no new entrance fees are imposed. Life care means a fully prepaid program that includes a contract promising care and a residence for life.

Life care agreements offer a prospective client a place to live, supported by various services that include specialized nursing care for a one-time substantial fee, plus a periodic (usually monthly) service charge.

Always ask these four specific questions when considering a life care agreement:

1. Under what circumstances does a resident have the right to cancel the agreement?

2. Under what circumstances will the entrance fee be refunded to the resident or the resident's estate?

3. When a refund is in order, what percentage of the entrance fee will the center refund?

4. Is payment of a refund conditioned on the unit being occupied?

Many like this model because there is no hassle with increases in entrance fees. Unfortunately, most senior adults find this model too expensive.

Exhibit 5 is a sample of a typical life care agreement utilized in a continuing care retirement community providing independent living.

In conclusion, you can easily find an agreement model with entrance requirements that meets your individual financial situation.

From the traditional lease agreement to the life care agreement is a broad spectrum. Because life care or tenancy agreements are more complex and are accompanied by substantial entrance fees or endowment payments, they can be confusing or too complex to the prospective resident. They may require more education to understand. But, the agreement that meets your needs and fits your budget is best for you.

Continuing Care Retirement Communities

A continuing care retirement community offers lifetime housing and a full range of health care and other services to older persons, including nursing care when it is needed. Housing may be high-rise buildings or individual apartments. In some areas, continuing care also is called life care.

Continuing care communities generally require a lump sum entrance fee, as well as monthly fees. Included in the basic fee is some kind of prepaid health care. Some continuing care facilities offer full health care benefits at no additional charge. Others require payment for some health care services or an additional payment after a certain number of days in the nursing home have passed.

Obviously, all continuing care communities are not alike. They vary not only in services, but also in fees. Discovering whether this type community fits your needs and lifestyle is the first step. Do not be shy about asking questions before you decide to move in. Use the questions on the following pages.

Checklist for Housing in Retirement Centers

Use the following questions as a simple, friendly checklist when considering various retirement centers:

❑ What are the sizes of the housing units?

❑ Do you provide home maintenance and repairs, and at what cost?

❑ Do you provide housekeeping services, and at what cost?

❑ Are gardening and ground services provided, and at what cost?

❑ Is there special housing for married couples?

❑ Are the residences furnished?

❑ Can I bring my own furnishings?

❑ What is done with my personal property if I must move elsewhere on the continuum of care campus?

❑ How does the monthly fee compare to the cost of renting a comparable apartment in the same vicinity?

❑ What are my rights as a tenant under the occupancy license?

❑ Can I be removed from my residence against my will? If so, under what circumstances?

❑ How long is the residence maintained in my absence (such as an indefinite stay in the nursing facility), and at what cost?

❑ What are my rights under state contract law? What agency regulates the law?

❑ Does this facility offer necessary services, such as food service, transportation, social and recreational activities, and assisted living?

Checklist for Health Care in Retirement Centers

Use the following questions to fully evaluate the health care provided by any retirement center you are considering:

❑ Is the health care facility located on the center's premises?

❑ Is the health care facility approved by Medicare and Medicaid? If not, who inspected and licensed the facility?

❑ Is each resident required or recommended to carry private supplementary insurance?

❑ Does the center accept Medicaid payment for other services?

❑ Is the nursing unit licensed as a skilled nursing facility?

❑ Does the health care facility offer preferential admission to residents of the campus?

❑ What is the ratio of nursing staff to residents?

❑ Are there nurses and physicians on call in the community 24 hours a day?

❑ Does this retirement center offer private rooms to patients in the nursing facility?

Financial Checklist for Retirement Centers

Use these questions to better understand the financial issues for you and for any retirement center you are considering:

❑ What is the entrance fee?

❑ Under what circumstances, if any, can it be refunded?

❑ What are the monthly fees? How are they calculated? What do they include?

❑ Under what conditions, if any, can the monthly fee be changed? Are these changes tied to predictable factors, such as the Consumer Price Index?

❑ What expenses do you expect each resident to cover?

❑ What organization or person actually owns this center?

❑ Is this center a proprietary (for profit) or nonprofit organization?

❑ Is this center sponsored by or affiliated with a larger organization?

❑ What are the legal, financial, moral, and ethical responsibilities of the owner to this center?

❑ Is this center financially independent?

❑ What are this center's financial reserves?

❑ Are the entrance fees held in reserve funds or used to meet current operating costs?

❑ How are monthly fees and residency affected by changes in marital status (widowhood or remarriage)?

❑ If you are considering a new facility, how many units were sold before construction began?

Checklist for Retirement Centers' Contracts

Use the following questions to assess the provisions of any retirement center's contract with its residents:

❑ What are this center's admissions policies?

❑ Do residents have any redress if or when the center's sponsor changes?

❑ How long is the grace period allowed for me to decide about entering this center?

❑ What are the provisions of the contract? How binding is it?

❑ Is the balance of my investment reimbursed to me or my family at the time of my withdrawal from the center or my death?

❑ Are there any stipulations about having guests in this center?

❑ What is this center's policy regarding residents who have financial difficulty meeting monthly fees?

Checklist for Community and Social Services in Retirement Centers

Use the following questions to discover the social and recreational options in any retirement center you are considering:

❑ What part do residents play in formulating this center's policies regarding its services?

❑ What recreational activities are provided and at what cost?

❑ Are any transportation services provided, and at what cost?

❑ Does this center provide any social workers or counseling services, and at what cost?

❑ Are there facilities appropriate for religious services or meetings? What restrictions, if any, are there to determine the denominations or other religious groups allowed access to these facilities?

❑ Are there any rebates for facilities or activities not used by a resident?

❑ Do residents have any input in menu planning?

❑ Are there arrangements for activities outside the center?

Making Your Decision

Your decision to select a particular retirement center probably will be determined primarily by your financial situation. Once you have settled the money issue, then the following practical concerns will help you finish the selection process:

- Physical appearance—regular maintenance of facilities, cleanliness, attractive grounds

- Security—alarm systems, emergency response plans, guards where necessary

- Safety—structures designed to strictest codes, handicap access, fire safety devices, mobility aids

- Recreational activities— multiple events planned each day, posted activities calendars

- Available services—meals; housekeeping; assisted living; laundry; transportation to doctors' offices, grocery stores, and banks

- Community spirit—friendly staff and residents

Obviously, the decision to move to a retirement center or community is multifaceted and is not easy. Start early in the planning process. Remember, senior adults often take six months to two years to finalize this decision. Once made, however, it can result in some of the most rewarding times older adults ever experience, a time when they can enjoy the conveniences of home with many of the amenities and services they have dreamed about their entire lives.

Personal Planning

Chapter 5
Assisted Living

Assisted living is a term used to describe assistance provided at home to accomplish the tasks of daily living. Assistance often provided includes housekeeping, laundry, limited maintenance, meal preparation, medication monitoring, bathing, grooming, shopping, transportation, and similar services. These services enable a person to remain independent at home longer than would have been possible without this assistance.

Assisted living is also referred to as home support or catered living. Whatever the terminology, assistance with daily living provides a tremendous advantage to older individuals to maintain their independence in the quiet and comfort of their homes. Generally, such services can be customized to fit any given situation.

Assisted living can be provided by family and friends. This is part of the caregiving concept in the home—providing necessary care designed specifically for another person.

Assisted living can also be procured through external agencies, such as home health agencies, transportation services, home-delivered meal services, or shopping services. One advantage of external agencies is their specific training in providing professional quality services. These agencies charge fees for services rendered, usually with a minimum charge, regardless of the level or amount of service.

Most retirement centers provide assisted living. One advantage in this setting is that the same staff generally provides all needed services. The familiarity of the one providing assistance is reassuring and comforting to the person receiving the service.

Estimates of elderly persons' needs for assistance with daily personal tasks—bathing, dressing, eating, moving from bed or chair, using the toilet—and for assistance with daily maintenance tasks such as housework, preparing meals, money management, shopping, telephone use, are as follows:

Age Group	Percentage Needing Help with Daily Personal Tasks	Percentage Needing Help with Daily Maintenance Tasks
65–74	17	21
75–84	28	33
85 and over	49	55

According to the American Association of Homes for the Aging, the limitations most frequently experienced by senior adults are the following:

Task	65-74 Yrs.	75-84 Yrs.	85+ Yrs.
Bathing	85%	90%	94%
Dressing	70%	76%	82%
Using the toilet	57%	60%	68%
Transferring from bed to chair	52%	60%	69%
Managing Incontinence	42%	55%	58%
Eating	33%	39%	44%

Perhaps the following summary of typical assisted living services will help you evaluate the viability of this option for yourself or your family member.

Services for Personal Needs

The extent to which persons can bathe, dress, feed, and groom themselves is highly important.

Personal hygiene is necessary for good health and affects one's general attitude toward life.

Bathing requires the ability to get to and from the bath, prepare the bath water, toiletries, and any special equipment needed for washing. Many older people begin to need assistance with this process.

Dressing requires the ability to put on, fasten, and take off items of clothing, a process difficult for persons with arthritis, recent stroke victims, or those recovering from certain types of surgeries. Many older people will need assistance with this process.

Eating requires the ability to get food, by any means, from the dish or glass into the body. This process is made more difficult if a person must be spoon-fed, tube-fed, or fed intravenously. Many self-help devices are on the market to assist persons with eating—larger handles on eating utensils and wider utensils that are easier to handle and to scoop food items.

Medication Monitoring Services

Obviously, it is important for individuals taking prescribed medications to administer them accurately. For different reasons, older people may need reminders to take their medications in the correct dosage, at the appropriate time, or to reorder medication when needed.

Monitoring services insure that persons take their medications appropriately. Individuals usually are able to self-administer their medications, but may need friendly reminders, encouragement, or observation in the process.

Equipment is available to assist people needing help with medication. Medisets are containers with seven spaces for storing multiple tablets to be taken in a week's time. It allows for placing the pills in the correct day and time slots for ease in completing a weekly medication regimen.

There are also plastic trays designed to hold insulin syringes filled with correct dosages. Trays can be marked morning or evening, and multiple trays can be used to complete daily injections.

Chore Services

Chore services offer help in and around the house, including minor repairs, heavy housekeeping, and yard work. Some people may not be able to adequately maintain their homes without assistance, even though they manage all of their personal needs.

Senior Centers

Senior centers offer a variety of social, health, nutritional, educational, and recreational services. They plan opportunities for older persons to gather socially. Many senior centers provide transportation from home to the center and to other activities in the community. Additionally, senior centers offer counseling, special trips, legal services, and advice on financial matters to their senior adult clientele.

Housekeeping Services

Housekeeping involves the ability to keep a house clean. Many older people merely need assistance with light housekeeping tasks on an intermittent basis. Housekeeping services would assist with or do dusting, sweeping, vacuuming, and washing dishes, as well as heavy cleaning chores performed less frequently as required.

Laundry Services

The process of sorting, washing, drying, ironing, and storing clean laundry can be difficult for some older persons because of the weight of clothes, both dry and wet, and the amount of time it takes to complete the laundry process. Usually, weekly laundry service is adequate unless an individual is incontinent.

Mobility and Transportation Services

Some senior adults gradually lose their ability for movement within their environments. The process of walking can be difficult, even depressing for some, and restricted or lost mobility is dreaded. Special equipment such as a walker or wheelchair provides some mobility. Mobility services offer senior adults the security of a person standing by or walking alongside them.

Transportation also involves the ability to drive one's own car as opposed to someone else providing the transportation. Some older people also need external transportation sources to get to their doctors' offices, banks, grocery stores, or drug stores. Many organizations provide this transportation, some even for free. In a retirement center setting, this service is usually free.

Companionship Services

The staff of companionship services provide social interaction, friendship, and activity-related functions for senior adults who need someone to talk to, write their letters, make certain phone calls, accompany them on a vacation or outing, or just assist them with shopping or other special needs.

This service gives older adults a greater sense of security and meets their need to socialize. Many senior adults are confined to their homes, and companionship services are just what they need to maintain independence and social skills.

Meal Preparation

Meal preparation services concentrate on providing nutritious meals on a consistent basis, from purchasing foods, preparing them for cooking, the actual cooking, and the cleaning up after meals. Many seniors do not eat appropriately because of the difficulty with meal preparation or the time involved. Also, their appetites diminish with age due to the loss of taste buds. Therefore, meal preparation is important for their health.

Organizations such as Meals On Wheels and other agencies provide nutritious meals on a daily basis for seniors. Persons are also available who will actually come into the home to prepare meals.

Friendly Visiting Services

Friendly visiting services provide regular visits to older persons who are lonely. Visits are made to homebound adults or to residents in institutions. Volunteers drop in regularly to do what any other concerned friend might do: sit and chat, write letters, run local errands, and listen.

Shopping Services

Shopping services are linked to

mobility and help older adults obtain needed items for themselves or their homes. Many organizations provide this type of service for homebound individuals. Shopping regularly for food and personal items is important to maintain personal health and hygiene. While visits to the bank or doctor may be less frequent, these are vitally important as well. Retirement centers offer these services as part of their normal fee schedules.

Telephone Reassurance Services

Telephone reassurance services enlist volunteers to make daily calls to persons living alone. A daily phone call by a regular caller at a prearranged time can serve as reassurance that all is well. The caller gives information on community activities and arranges for special services if help is needed. If the older person does not answer the phone, the caller is trained to alert neighbors or police. This service is usually provided by church, civic, or other organizations.

Chore and Maintenance Services

Chore and maintenance services handle light maintenance and routine household chores. Many senior adults must relocate to other types of housing because of their inability to perform these routine tasks. External assistance can be obtained from a variety of sources. The yellow pages list organizations providing maintenance services. Other resources may include churches, civic groups, or other service organizations.

Fiduciary Services

Fiduciary services handle others' routine financial matters such as balancing a checkbook, paying bills, filing insurance claims, and investing money.

Fiduciary services can be performed by family, friends, banks, home health agencies, or retirement centers. They are most effective when performed as the need arises.

Summary

The assisted living services described in this chapter enable persons to function independently, remain in their home environment, avoid placement in a higher level of institutional care, and avoid depleting financial resources on costlier care.

Too many people are placed needlessly in higher levels of care; in fact, 50 percent of all nursing home admissions could be prevented through a properly planned and delivered assisted living program. Be sure to explore all avenues open to you and your family for assisted living before a decision is made to relocate.

Personal Planning

CHAPTER 6
RESIDENTIAL CARE

Residential care is typically associated with a retirement center. In some states residential care is also called supervisory care or catered living. All the terms are synonymous.

Residential care offers semi-independent living for those who need some help to manage each day and its needs. It is the ideal answer for elderly people who are no longer able to live alone yet wish to maintain their independence. Group living in a homelike atmosphere is facilitated by qualified staff on duty 24 hours a day for the safety, security, and assistance residents need.

Residential care provides individuals room, board, and general supervision. Residents must be able to care for themselves and move about without the help of another person.

This type of care may be licensed or unlicensed, depending upon the state and the individual choice of the owner. Licensed facilities come under closer scrutiny with specific rules and regulations to be met. They also are surveyed or inspected annually to insure they meet a state's standards of care.

Most states prescribe the following criteria for those receiving residential care services.

1. Mobility: Residents must be independently able to walk, with or without assistive devices, or independently mobile in a wheelchair, including transfer to other areas.

2. Eating: Residents must be able to feed themselves. Special diets as ordered by a physician can be delivered by the staff.

3. Bathing: Residents must bathe themselves, although staff is allowed to supervise and assist if needed.

4. Continence: Residents must be continent or able to provide their own care for an indwelling catheter, colostomy, or disposable briefs.

5. Medication and treatment: Staff members are allowed to remind residents of their medication and bring it to them, but it must be self-administered or overseen by home health or other outpatient services.

6. Mental: Residents are mentally stable and capable of knowing reality.

7. Social: Residents may be forgetful or exhibit minor judgment defects in social settings. When this occurs, staff guidance is allowed.

8. Emotional: Residents are emotionally stable, usually capable of socializing and communicating.

Relatives usually make the choice of residential care placement when a family member is no longer able to continue living at home or needs a safe and secure environment for some reason. Most commonly, the inability to manage one or more daily living tasks mentioned in Chapter 1 of this book is the reason most seek residential care placement.

Basic residential care services will include:

- General 24-hour supervision

- Three nutritious meals per day

- Snacks offered between meals

- Assistance in crisis situations

- Supervision of medication and personal hygiene needs

- Scheduled activities and outings

- Housekeeping and laundry services

- Emergency call systems in each room and bathroom

- Approved fire and safety systems

- Personal laundry services

Rates for residential care are usually based on a daily rate for semi-private or private rooms. Some facilities allow paying extra to convert a semi-private room into a private room. In general, rates vary between $35 and $55 per day depending upon accommodations, type of room, and geographic location.

Usually, payment for residential care can be made two ways, depending upon the payment source. First, payment can be made from an individual's personal resources. Secondly, payment can be made by Medicaid, assuming the facility is certified as a Medicaid provider and accepts Medicaid as a payment source. Contact your local welfare office or state human services division to find out if you qualify for Medicaid payments.

Staff members are specially trained to meet the distinct needs of older persons. They are also trained in CPR for emergencies. However, when deciding about residential care, observe the general attitude of the staff, too. They should be friendly, courteous, and helpful, exhibiting genuine concern and care for residents.

Exhibit 6 is a sample of a typical residential care agreement used by a retirement center.

To choose the best possible retirement center care, you must recognize your needs. Take into account your lifestyle, availability of help from family and friends, and the types of services available in your community. Answering the following questions can assist you in making the right choice.

Is there a problem with:

• Taking care of daily needs such as bathing, dressing, or using the bathroom?

• Moving around safely, either walking or in a wheelchair?

• Planning, preparing, and/or eating nutritious meals?

• Taking medicine as ordered by the doctor?

• Confusion, memory loss, or mood changes that interfere with daily life?

• Safety or feeling secure?

• Isolation from daily contact with others?

• Getting to and from doctors' appointments or places such as shopping centers, social functions, or church?

• Handling money and paying bills?

On the basis of your answers to these questions, you will recognize the type of services and care you need. The first step is to identify the activities you can manage plus those needs requiring the help of another person.

Carefully note: residential care residents have what is called "Resident Rights." These special policies and procedures insure them the following rights.

1. To manage their personal affairs: Residents have the right to manage their own personal affairs. Some residents may authorize the resident manager to assume responsibility for handling their financial affairs in writing.

2. To be provided effective means of communication: Residents shall be provided an effective method of communicating with staff if language or culture impedes normal, daily communication.

3. To possess and enjoy personal civil rights: Residents shall continue to possess and enjoy the personal civil rights granted to all citizens. Residents will be encouraged to exercise the rights of free speech, voting, and engaging in political activities outside the facility.

4. Personal privacy: Residents shall have the right to refuse or agree to receive visitors and to arrive and depart from the center without personal interference from any person. Conversely, residents must notify the management when they leave the premises and when they return. All resident mail shall be opened only by the resident.

5. *To be treated with dignity and respect:* Residents shall be treated at all times with regard for their individuality and privacy and shall be free from any form of medical, psychological, or physical abuse.

6. *To have access to stored personal property:* Residents shall have access to a secure container where their valuable personal property may be safely stored in the facility.

7. *To be informed of rights, rates, and service:* Residents shall receive complete information on residents' rights, the center's rates, and services available at the facility. Also, oral and written notice shall be given at least two weeks prior to any changes in rates or services.

8. *To be discharged upon request:* Residents shall have the right to be discharged upon their own request or the request of their family or legal representative.

Many times residential care centers have a waiting list of interested prospective residents. Find out from the facility or agency how long the waiting list is, if they make exceptions for special cases, and a realistic estimate of how long the wait will be. In the meantime, remember your family, friends, and the myriad external agencies that are valuable resources for help each day.

Personal Planning

CHAPTER 7

CONTINUUM OF CARE

Continuum of care is an alternative that packages key services, including housing, health care, and social services to the elderly in one community. More specifically, a continuum of care retirement community provides: 1) independent living units—either apartments, studios, or efficiencies; 2) assisted living services to residents; 3) residential care services; and 4) a range of health care and social services from skilled to intermediate to personal care, all available on the same premises.

One facility may provide all, or only a mixture, of these four levels of care. A true continuum of care retirement community will provide all four. This means that everything can be provided on one campus.

The concept of a continuum of care was developed to meet the older person's need for an independent way of life and to give him/her the security of guaranteed affordable housing, health care, and other services throughout their later years—even as their health changes—without leaving the same campus or environment, beloved friends, and familiar staff.

There are distinct advantages to a continuum of care retirement community.

Maintaining Relationships with Family and Friends

One of the most traumatic experiences for anyone is to relocate physically away from family and friends. This is particularly true for most senior adults because loneliness and a need for companionship are two of their prime concerns. If changes in health status are accommodated without relocating, then senior adults gain assurance about the stability of their world and much of their anxiety about health and aging is removed.

Studies show that regular contact with family and friends promotes healthful living and contributes to more complete recovery from illness. The elderly pay a price, particularly with their health, when they must leave behind family and friends.

Avoidance of Physical Relocation

Physical relocation—moving—is stressful to anyone at any age. Senior adults encounter great difficulty in completing a physical relocation, and once is often enough to move in the later years. The process of determining what furniture to take, planning to live in less square footage, selling extra furniture and personal items, and deciding what to do with special keepsakes all cause much confusion and stress. Costs run high with both short- or long-distance moving and need careful consideration.

Temporary Rehabilitation and Care

Rehabilitation after a stroke or recovery from surgery or serious illnesses are good selling points for continuum of care campuses. After hospitalization, older people often require care and treatment not available in an independent living setting. Therefore, a continuum of care campus can meet those needs because it offers residential care and nursing home care.

Residents can move between independent living, residential care, and nursing care as needed without having to leave the campus. This is a particularly appealing feature for older couples when one spouse must enter a nursing home, or for single or widowed residents who wish to and need to remain close to friends.

Financial Stability

Continuum of care retirement centers tend to be more financially stable than those relying on only one type of care for their profit margin. One of the major reasons many retirement communities have gone out of business is that they did not diversify their services to the elderly. Many senior adults have invested their financial resources in one facility offering only minimum levels of care only to lose great sums of money because they did not choose a continuum of care retirement center.

Cost Less

Because of the diversity in the services provided and offered, continuum of care retirement centers tend to be less expensive than other retirement centers. From an operating standpoint, adequate excess revenue over expenses is easier to accumulate in a continuum of care retirement center. Therefore, rates and fees are usually priced lower.

Continuum of Care Is the Consumer Choice

Studies indicate that senior adults choosing retirement housing prefer continuum of care retirement centers. Generally, they prefer to make only one move when they leave their homes. In choosing a continuum of care retirement center, they do not have to move as their health status changes because the variety of services and levels of care needed are offered in one setting.

I am a strong supporter of the continuum of care concept. Residents seem to adjust sooner to their new environment. Rehabilitation from illnesses, surgeries, and other health problems occurs more quickly. Residents have a greater sense of security and less anxiety in this kind of environment. If a continuum of care retirement center becomes one of your choices for retirement housing and health care, all other things being equal, I strongly suggest that you make this choice.

Section 3
Nursing Home Care

CHAPTER 8
CHOOSING A NURSING HOME

The decision to seek nursing home placement can be a difficult experience for everyone concerned. It can mean loss of one's lifestyle and of important things that help define an individual—one's own home, personal possessions, and daily routines.

Once the decision is made for you to enter a nursing home, it becomes important to select the home that is right for you and learn how to adjust to living there.

Some people who need nursing home placement have the luxury of time and the availability of several nursing homes with vacancies from which to choose. For many others, however, the need for nursing home placement is more immediate, and the openings in nursing homes are scarce, leaving little opportunity for planning the move and selecting the best place.

By knowing ahead of time how to look for a facility that best meets your needs, you will have more control over this situation.

One of the most difficult decisions any person ever faces is the prospect of getting a loved one in a nursing home. Over the years, media coverage about the poor nursing homes—ones with abuse, inappropriate care, understaffing—has created a negative image for all nursing homes. The truth is that most nursing homes give quality nursing care, offer multiple activities, provide good food, and are very clean.

During the early 1970s, I served as Generalist Surveyor for the Mississippi State Board of Health. My job was to inspect hospitals, nursing homes, and home health agencies for licensure and certification for Medicare and Medicaid programs. During my tenure with the State Board of Health, I inspected hundreds of nursing homes, representing all levels of care, ownership, and types of licensure.

For over 20 years, I have served in an administrative or management capacity for delivering health care in hospitals and nursing homes. Therefore, I understand health care facilities from an inspector's point of view, as well as from a management point of view. While the perspective may be different, the elements for delivering quality nursing care and administrating such a facility remain the same. In this chapter, I will share some basic conclusions I have reached from my experience which I trust will be beneficial to you when choosing a nursing home.

You must visit and compare several nursing homes to find the one to best meet your needs. Only by seeing these nursing homes can you get a true picture of the levels of care they offer and the people who provide the care.

The following questions include points to consider in selecting a nursing home. They can help you know what to look for and ask about when you visit a nursing home, and also how to size up a nursing home and compare it with others you have visited.

1. Is the facility currently licensed by the state to provide the level of care you need?

Specifically, is the nursing home licensed for skilled care?

intermediate care?

personal care?

2. Will the nursing home give you a copy of its admission agreement and patient care policies to study?

Are there other agreements, contracts, or forms you must sign before admission?

3. Is a statement of residents' rights clearly posted?

Does the facility staff protect these rights?

4. Is the atmosphere warm, pleasant and cheerful?

Are the rooms well lighted, well ventilated, and kept at a comfortable temperature?

Is each resident provided a reading light, comfortable chair, and a closet and drawers for personal belongings?

5. Are family and friends encouraged to visit?

   Are there indoor and/or outdoor places for private visits with family and friends?

   What are the visiting hours?

   Are residents allowed to leave the nursing home with family and friends?

6. Do the residents look cared for and generally content?

   Are they dressed in street clothes?

   Are residents allowed to:

   • decorate their own rooms?

   • keep a few of their own possessions?

   • choose their own bedtimes?

   How does the nursing home select roommates?

   Is there a screen or partition available between beds for privacy?

7. Are toilet and bathing facilities easy for disabled residents to use?

   Is the nursing home built to accommodate wheelchairs?

   Are grab bars and safety devices available?

8. Is an emergency evacuation plan posted in a visible place?

   Does the nursing home have safety devices such as smoke detectors, a sprinkler system, fire extinguishers, and fire doors?

   How often are fire and disaster drills practiced?

   Are the hallways kept clear for a safe evacuation?

9. Is the general appearance clean and odor free?

   Do you detect the use of deodorant sprays to cover up or mask odors?

10. What provisions are made for:

    • calling a doctor when a problem occurs?

    • medical emergencies?

    • dental care?

    • foot care?

    • filling prescriptions?

    • routine medical appointments?

11. Is the dining room clean, comfortable and attractive?

    Are residents encouraged to eat in the dining room?

    Do residents who need it get assistance to and from the dining room?

    What is the meal schedule?

    What kinds of foods are included in the menus?

    Are snacks offered and served when requested?

    Do residents who need help with eating get it?

    Are visitors allowed to eat with residents?

12. How does the home encourage residents, their families, and their friends to assist in the residents' care?

    Does the nursing home encourage suggestions from residents and their families?

Is family involved in developing a resident's plan of care?

13. Is there a variety of interesting social, recreational, and cultural activities planned?

Where is the schedule of activities posted?

Is there a variety of activities scheduled on a daily basis?

Do you see residents participating in the activities during your visit?

Is there a lounge or community room for residents to use?

Are residents using this room during your visit?

14. Do residents have opportunities to attend religious services and activities of their own faith?

What is the policy for visiting by ministers?

Does the facility have an inhouse chaplain?

15. What is the basic monthly charge?

What services are included in this charge?

Is there an additional charge for:

- personal laundry?

- medical supplies?

- transportation?

- pharmaceuticals?

- therapy services?

- hair grooming?

- activities?

- telephone?

- cable?

16. What is the refund policy if a resident is discharged, goes to the hospital, or dies? Is this policy included in the agreement?

17. Do residents, volunteers, and staff speak favorably and freely about the facility?

18. Are the staff members cheerful and courteous?

Do they demonstrate genuine affection for the residents?

Do they smile and speak respectfully when talking with the residents?

Is the general attitude of the staff friendly and helpful?

19. Can the nursing home provide special services when ordered by a doctor such as special diets, physical therapy, speech therapy, occupational therapy, intravenous medication, oxygen treatment, or tube feeding?

20. Does the nursing home help the residents in finding available financial resources?

If Medicare, Medicaid, Veterans Administration, county or private insurance payment is contemplated, is the nursing home certified to accept placement?

In addition to thoroughly answering these questions, pay careful attention to two other key factors when selecting a nursing home:

- Licensure deficiencies and quality rating; and

- Staffing levels in nursing service.

1. Licensure Deficiencies and Quality Rating

All nursing homes are licensed by the state. As a part of their licensure, and relicensure on an annual basis, they are inspected by some state agency. Most states assign this task to the Department of Health and Human Services.

Inspections are performed on at least an annual basis. The Statement of Deficiencies is then sent to each facility, and they have 10 working days to develop and submit a Plan of Correction in writing to the inspecting agency. The Statement of Deficiencies and Plan of Correction are public documents and are to be posted in a prominent place in each facility. A facility may have multiple reinspections to insure that deficiencies have been corrected to the satisfaction of the inspecting agency. These written reports will also be posted in the facility.

I would recommend that you carefully review these documents because they will indicate the quality of the facility and the overall scope of any deficiencies. Be sure to read the Plan of Correction because it will indicate the actions the facility intended to make to correct the deficiencies. Dates when the corrections occurred will be marked. While the number of deficiencies cited does indicate a home's quality or lack thereof, the types of deficiencies are more important. Those involving nursing care, quality of food, residents' rights, and sanitation or cleanliness should be your greatest concern.

In addition to the Statement of Deficiencies and Plan of Correction posted in the facility, you may find a quality rating assigned by the state to the nursing home. If you do not see the rating posted, be sure to ask if the nursing home has received one. While states do differ, the highest level rating usually given is: "Substantially exceeds licensure standards," which means exactly what it says. The facility is operating at a level substantially above the state's standards for licensed nursing home care.

2. Staffing Levels in Nursing Service

In general, the number of staff scheduled in the nursing department dictates the quality of care given to each resident. Therefore, this number is important to know.

Most facilities express nurse staffing in terms of nursing hours per patient day. This is calculated by dividing the number of daily nursing hours scheduled for all shifts by the number of residents in the facility.

Suppose the result is 2.5 nursing

hours per patient day. This means that enough staff is scheduled to give every resident 2.5 hours of direct, hands-on nursing care by staff. Remember, licensed nurses and nursing assistants are on duty 24 hours a day to respond to any need.

Staff levels required in nursing homes vary among the states based on their licensure status. Refer to Chapter 2 in the glossary, and you will find that nursing homes can provide four levels of care (licensure status): sub-acute care, skilled nursing care, intermediate nursing care, and personal care. Each of these levels of care has a minimum nursing staff required in order to meet licensure standards. Again, states will vary the minimum nursing staff required. Note the chart at the bottom of the page.

Many nursing homes have multiple levels of care and place residents in specific wings designed for these levels of care. In other words, they group residents with similar needs requiring similar care.

I recommend that you ask the facility's administrator or director of nursing services about their daily staffing levels for the type of care you or your family member needs. Talk to them about their philosophy regarding staffing. Quality nursing homes will staff higher than the minimum required by the state, as much as one-third to one-half nursing hours per patient day higher than the state minimum. This allocation gives sufficient staff to assure quality care, but preserves a cost efficient operation and encourages optimum work done by the staff.

Many times nursing homes have a waiting list, so choose more than one to suit your needs and put your name on the waiting list. In the meantime, check on alternative community services such as adult day care, respite care, or home health care services to meet your immediate needs.

It is not easy deciding what to do when you have a health problem or disability and can no longer live independently. Accepting the reality that you, or a person who is close to you, are no longer able to live

Levels of Care per Patient	Daily Nursing Hours
Sub-acute care	2.5
Skilled nursing care	2.5
Intermediate nursing care	2.0
Personal nursing care	1.5

independently is difficult at best. Planning the best possible care involves choosing from the available nursing homes in your community.

In order to choose the best possible care, you must recognize your specific need level. Take into account your lifestyle, the availability of help from family and friends, and the types of services available in your community.

It will take time to gather information and plan appropriate care. Rely on the people who can help you with information, assistance, and emotional support. Your family and friends, doctor, clergy, staff from social service agencies, and many other concerned individuals are all resources you may call on for help. The choices are often bewildering, and you do not need to face them alone.

Many people feel concern about what has happened and worry about their future. These feelings are normal. Recognizing your feelings is important. Learning what it is you are feeling and why you are feeling it helps you deal with the emotions you experience. It may be helpful to talk about your feelings with a relative, friend, favorite minister, or counselor. It will take time to adjust. Then accepting your feelings will help you move ahead, plan for nursing home care and adapt to the changes in your life.

Everyone involved in choosing nursing home services shares a common concern: Did I make the right choice? By taking time to learn about nursing home services, you will be able to make a more informed decision.

CHAPTER 9
ADMITTING A NURSING HOME RESIDENT

Admitting a resident into a nursing home usually occurs because all other alternatives for health care have been exhausted. The prospective resident requires 24-hour supervision and care by licensed nurses on a continuing basis.

The following factors are compelling indicators an older person likely needs nursing home placement and care:

- High level of chronic disability

- Family members unavailable or unable to provide help

- Deteriorating mental functions

- Much time is spent in a hospital or other health facility

While I would be among the first to say nursing home care should be a consideration, many persons living in nursing homes do not need to be there. This situation occurs because people do not know the other options available:

- Home health care

- Adult day care

- Residential care

- Caregiving within the home

- Assisted living

- Group homes

These options are fully discussed in Chapter 4.

However, if these alternatives are not appropriate, nursing home placement should be the choice. The deciding factor is more often the need for appropriate care rather than whether adult children can care for their parents. If you choose your nursing home under the guidelines outlined in Chapter 8, you can feel confident that the care will be good.

The admissions process can be traumatic for the older adults and especially for their family members. The purpose of this chapter is to address issues you will face before, during, and after admission to a nursing home. Advance knowledge of the process will prepare you for the actual event. Additionally, making informed decisions appropriate for your needs removes some of the trying, emotional moments and improves objectivity throughout the process.

The admissions process includes the following 11 steps:

1. Choosing a nursing home physician

2. Planning for the admission

3. Arriving at the nursing home

4. Completing admissions forms

5. Deciding on advanced directives

6. Learning about resident responsibilities

7. Choosing a pharmacy

8. Getting to know the staff

9. Making use of personal belongings

10. Getting the resident adjusted

11. Dealing with the guilt of nursing home placement

1. Choosing a Nursing Home Physician
Hopefully, your regular physician will continue to provide your medical care during your stay in the nursing home. However, many physicians do not practice medicine in nursing homes. Therefore, you may have to choose a new physician to take care of you.

First, find out which physicians practice medicine in your nursing home. You should be able to obtain a list of physicians on the medical staff of the facility from the home's administrator, director of nursing service, or director of admissions. These individuals can assist you in making your choice.

Some important questions to ask when finding a new physician are:

• Does the physician care for several residents in the facility?

• Does the physician make routine visits as required by the Medicare or Medicaid guidelines?

• Does the physician have an on-call system so that some physician is available in emergency situations?

• Does the physician participate in assuring the quality of the facility?

• Does the physician encourage patients to openly discuss feelings and talk about personal concerns?

• Does the physician seem to automatically prescribe drugs for symptoms rather than uncover underlying causes of medical problems?

- Does the physician attribute problems to "old age," for example, instead of properly evaluating patients' concerns?

- Does the physician explain the nature of medical conditions in simple language?

- Does the physician respond promptly to telephone calls?

A good relationship between doctor and patient is built upon open lines of communication. This is particularly true in the case of a nursing home physician.

Sometimes the medical director for the facility is a good choice for your doctor. He or she is a paid consultant to the facility and usually has the patients' well-being and the facility's good in mind. He or she is usually the best medical supporter of the facility and responds quickly in the event of problems, and the person on whom the facility administration relies for medical guidance and assistance.

Physicians are required to visit their patients at specific intervals and to complete certain elements of their medical records on a timely basis. Therefore, engage a physician who will cooperate with the facility and meet its requirements as well as those outlined by Medicare, Medicaid, or other funding programs you may use.

You want a physician who understands nursing home care and the needs of the elderly. Not all enjoy treating geriatric residents. Be sure to select one who does.

2. Planning for the Admission

Prior to admission, certain requirements must be met. If the patient has been in a hospital, the social worker or discharge planner from the hospital will work directly with the nursing home's director of admissions to obtain all the hospital's medical information and physician's orders. Certain diagnostic tests such as X rays and lab work must be completed within a specific number of days prior to admission into a nursing home. This process is coordinated by the social worker or discharge planner of the hospital.

If the patient is coming from another nursing home, generally the admissions process is coordinated by the receiving nursing home, and the dismissing nursing home cooperates, insuring a smooth transfer. Copies of medical records and other material is sent to the receiving nursing home to facilitate the admissions process.

If the prospective resident is coming from home, family members need to work closely with the director of admissions of the nursing home. He or she will explain all the various requirements for admission, assist with the necessary documentation, and oversee the entire process.

Remember, the nursing home will benefit financially from your nursing home stay. Therefore, you should rely on them to assist you with planning for admission.

Typically, many nursing homes have no beds available, or their bed turnover rate is minimal. Therefore, begin early to plan for an eventual nursing home placement. If the facility has a waiting list, place your name on it as soon as possible. Know early in the process whether the nursing home takes Medicare, Medicaid, or other types of primary or supplemental funding. Many nursing homes only accept private pay residents and not any third party payments.

3. Arrival at the Nursing Home

Arriving at the nursing home can be traumatic, particularly if the new resident does not want to go there. However, the staff can make arrival easier if they know in advance that the new resident is apprehensive. Typically, admission is a good experience because the staff welcomes the new resident and makes the admission as easy as possible.

Upon arrival, the resident is taken to his or her room and oriented to the various features of the room and any special equipment. He or she learns how to raise and lower the bed, where to store clothes, how to work the emergency pull cord or button connected to the nurses' station, and is made aware in general of all aspects of the new surroundings.

The newcomer in a semi-private room is introduced to his or her new roommate. Even though most people believe a private room is best, experience shows that nursing home residents actually do better in semi-private rooms. Senior adults enjoy visiting with others, having

company, and feeling the security of others in the room. Therefore, you should determine what is best for the resident regarding the choice of a room.

4. Completing the Forms for Admission

The resident, family members, and/or sponsor have to complete many forms at admission. Sometimes, this can be done prior to admission, and I suggest doing that. It can make the day of admission more enjoyable for the resident and his or her family members.

Exhibit 7 is a typical Record of Admission for nursing home care. As you can see, it contains three major sections: 1) Patient Identification Summary, 2) Admission Summary, and 3) Discharge Summary. Upon admission, general information is obtained in sections one and two for use by the nursing home staff and physician.

Exhibit 8 is a sample admission agreement for nursing home care. It outlines the financial aspects of the nursing home stay—the room and board charges, ancillary charges, and other billing statements in accordance with the nursing home policies and procedures.

Other forms are required such as acknowledgment of receipt of resident rights, resident grievance procedures, choice of pharmacy to use, various policies and procedures, and release of information consent. Depending on the payment source, some of these forms may have to be signed.

A resident history form generally is completed at the time of admission so the staff will know more about the new resident. This information is helpful in the delivery of care and in coordinating services and activities. The more information the staff knows about the personality and background of the resident, the better they serve.

5. Deciding on Advanced Directives

What are advanced directives? They could be a living will or a durable power of attorney for health care. Either document allows you to give directions about future medical care.

It is your right to accept or refuse medical care. Advance directives protect this right if you ever become mentally or physically unable to choose or communicate your wishes because of an injury or illness. Advance directives help:

- You to protect your right to make medical choices that can affect your life;

- Your family to avoid the responsibility and stress of making difficult decisions; and

- Your physician adhere to guidelines you have settled on for your care.

Advanced directives can protect people in extreme conditions—those unable to communicate due to irreversible brain damage or brain disease, permanent coma, or a terminal illness that could lead to brain damage or loss of consciousness.

Advanced directives can limit life-prolonging measures such as cardiopulmonary resuscitation (CPR), intravenous (IV) therapy, feeding tubes, respirators, defibrillation, and dialysis. Advanced directives can also address pain relief—either requesting it or refusing it. These directives may enable patients to make their feelings known about these matters.

There are generally two types of advance directives. First, a living will sets out written instructions explaining your wishes regarding health care should you develop a terminal condition. They are called "living" wills because they take effect while you are still alive. Second, a durable power of attorney is a written document naming a person (called a proxy) to make decisions for you if you become unable to make them yourself.

Exhibit 9 is a typical living will; **Exhibit 10** is a typical durable power of attorney regarding health care. Both documents can be used in any health care facility.

Even if your state does not currently recognize living wills, you may want to draw one up, in addition to a durable power of attorney, to express your wishes as completely and specifically as possible. If living wills are accepted in your state, it may have special forms to use.

Let your values be your guide when creating advance directives. The following statements appear in any such documents. Determine which ones express how you might think or feel if you were near death:

- To die without pain or suffering

- To make my own decisions when I am able

- To leave my family with good memories

- Not to burden my family with difficult decisions

- To act according to my religious beliefs

- To be with loved ones at death

Plan to discuss your feelings and responses with your family and friends, physician, minister, and attorney.

Special issues to consider:

- Do not resuscitate orders (DNR)
  A DNR order allows you to refuse future attempts to restore heartbeat. This is also known as a "no code." Discuss this option with your family and physician.

- Organ donation
  Advance directives state your wishes to donate only specific organs or your entire body after death.

- Specific treatments
  In addition to pain control, you may request or refuse tube feeding and other medical procedures.

Whatever you decide about advanced directives should be reviewed on a regular basis.

The director of admissions of the nursing home will ask if you have advanced directives, a living will, or a durable power of attorney. These protective documents honor your wishes about many important matters.

6. Learning Resident Responsibilities

Upon admission, you will be informed of certain resident responsibilities during your stay in the nursing home:

- Meeting financial obligations;

- Furnishing adequate clothing;

- Securing money and valuables;

- Judicious use of the home's resources;

- Storage of food;

- Personal conduct and respecting the rights of others; and

- Removal of possessions.

Residents and families who habitually fail to meet these responsibilities are first counseled.

Continued failure to meet these obligations results in discharge from the facility. Other resident responsibilities may be imposed by individual nursing homes.

7. Choosing a Pharmacy

Choosing a pharmacy to provide medications during your stay in a nursing home is an important decision. Medicines are important in recovery from health problems and in continued health; therefore, choose a pharmacy that can provide your medications in a prompt, cost efficient manner.

Important questions to ask:

- Does the pharmacy provide 24-hour, 7-day a week service?

- Does the pharmacist visit the nursing home to review the drug regimen of each resident as required by law?

- Does the pharmacist discuss any drug interactions with the staff and the resident?

- Does the pharmacist keep a drug profile on each resident so that no unnecessary use of medication increases over time or begins to counteract other medicines being taken?

- Does the pharmacist dispense medications in keeping with the administrative policies of the nursing home?

Usually, nursing homes have a specific contract with a pharmacy that meets all the above requirements. If the nursing home has its own pharmacy, it is a good idea to use it—it is convenient, and the pharmacist is familiar with the staff, policies, and procedures. Be sure to check whether the drug prices at the facility are competitive.

8. Getting to Know the Staff

The more you are committed to knowing the staff on a friendly and professional basis, the better they will meet your needs or those of your family member. Perhaps that statement surprises you, but it is true. Residents and family members with a positive attitude toward the nursing home and its staff experience a more positive environment.

Nobody likes people who are constant complainers or have nothing positive to say. Be friendly with the staff. Get to know them by name. Speak to them In turn, they will be more responsive to your needs, suggestions, and concerns.

9. Using Personal Belongings

New residents need their familiar belongings. Be sure to bring basic clothing so that dressing each day feels like being at home.

Most facilities allow some personal furniture, such as a television, radio, favorite chair, and family pictures. These are also important to make the nursing home room seem more like their home.

Discuss the use of personal belongings with the director of admissions of the nursing home.

He or she will guide you with specific recommendations and instructions.

10. Getting the Resident Adjusted

Each new resident needs a certain amount of time to adjust and become acclimated to the facility. The length of time for adjustment varies with each resident. New residents sometimes are confused after being transferred from their home or from another facility. It is very important to have family and/or friends available at admission to help the new resident get settled into his or her room and new setting.

11. Dealing with the Guilt of Nursing Home Placement

Life is full of struggles and hard decisions. Perhaps no moment is so guilt-ridden or anxiety-causing as the nursing home quandary. It is one of life's toughest decisions.

One of the most feared events is placing a loved one in a nursing home. Unfortunately, this fear has been created by the poor reputation of a few nursing homes reported in detail by the media—physical abuse of residents, filthy living conditions, poor nursing care, residents lying in feces, residents being restrained in bed, and inadequate staffing.

Nursing homes are also portrayed as the last place anyone would want to go—and the last place one will ever live!

The truth is, the majority of nursing homes are well-managed, well-staffed, provide quality food, and provide excellent nursing care.

The media seem to focus on the negatives, thus creating a negative image for the entire industry. I have inspected and surveyed hundreds of nursing homes in several states. Very few are the inferior facilities like those portrayed by the media.

A statistic that the general public does not know is that 75 percent of all nursing home admissions are discharged alive to other places. This means that the majority of nursing home residents are rehabilitated to the extent they can receive a lower level of care or be discharged to go home. Twenty-five percent of all nursing home residents pass away while living in the nursing home. The average length of residency is two to three years.

Regardless of how good nursing homes are, most people still experience a deep sense of guilt when placing a loved one in a nursing home.

The guilt often is accompanied by depression that is caused by the sense of guilt, feelings of anxiety, hopelessness, sadness, and worry. The fact that the individual is institutionalized adds to the depression.

Studies show that the greatest guilt and depression occur in spouses who have to place their husband or wife in a nursing home, followed by daughters. Sons were the least demoralized by putting a parent into a nursing home, though having a mentally confused parent bothered them more than it did the others.

All these are natural feelings!

The fact that they are natural feelings should help you overcome your guilt in time.

Most nursing homes have family support groups that assist with any guilt you feel. Additionally, family, friends, clergy, and staff from the social services department can provide assistance and emotional support. You should feel free to discuss your feelings with the nursing staff in the facility. They can share health care information that can often relieve the anxiety and emotional stress.

Finally, talk to spouses and family members of other residents. They can be an encouragement to you. Remember, it is a natural response and feeling. You do not have to face the guilt and depression alone. "God is our refuge and strength, a very present help in trouble" (Ps. 46:1).

CHAPTER 10
REALISTIC EXPECTATIONS FOR A NURSING HOME

There are many misconceptions about nursing homes and the care provided by these facilities. Settling on realistic expectations for a nursing home helps residents and their family members to adapt better to an institutional setting and environment. Some of the more common misconceptions about nursing homes are dispelled in this chapter.

One-on-One Care

Many residents are admitted to a nursing home from a home environment where caregiving has been on a one-on-one, 24-hour a day basis that met their needs almost immediately. This caregiving expectation often carries over into a nursing home; and when it is not met, many residents and family members do not feel adequate care is being rendered.

You must understand that quality care in a nursing home is rendered in a different manner and at a different level. Most nursing homes are licensed to provide care known as skilled nursing care—a minimum 2.5 nursing hours per patient per day. This means there is enough nursing staff to provide direct, one-on-one care to each resident a total of 2.5 hours during a 24-hour period. Actual, direct patient care is determined on an individual basis by the care needs of each resident. However, the facility schedules staff based on the required 2.5 nursing hours per patient per day. The response time is more limited than what you expect in a hospital or certainly in a caregiving situation, but the quality of care is high.

It is equally important to know that licensed and nonlicensed nursing staff are available in the facility on a 24-hour a day, 7-day a week basis to respond to the needs and emergencies of residents. Professional staff, technically trained to perform a multitude of skilled tasks, are available to meet the medical needs of each resident.

The underlying issues prompting this misconception are response time and one-on-one care. Family members often place unrealistic expectations on the nursing staff because of misunderstandings over these issues. Nursing homes just cannot provide the same amount of personal care as one could give at home, but they do provide more skilled, professional care available 24-hours every day. So the final question or decision is: Does the resident require professional care and medical attention that only can be provided in an institutional type setting? If so, then the medical, rehabilitative, and support care the resident needs outweighs the desire for immediate, personal care for the tasks of daily living.

Use of Restraints

The use of physical or chemical restraints in a hospital or nursing home is controversial. A variety of physical restraints are available. Their purpose is to provide an extra measure of protection and safety for a resident. Restraints generally prevent falls and serve as a safeguard to maintain IVs, feeding tubes, and other medical equipment necessary to care for and treat residents.

Chemical restraints are less visible to an untrained eye. These are medications ordered by physicians and administered by the nursing staff. The sole purpose of controlling behavior chemically is to insure an extra measure of protection and safety for a resident, just as physical restraints do.

A few facilities have abused the use of both types of restraints to offset inadequate levels of nurse staffing. This should never be the case.

Most nursing facilities attempt to have a "restraint free" environment. While I agree with this philosophy and ultimate goal, the reality is that it will probably never be totally realized because some residents will always need such protection for their health and safety.

In your visits to any nursing home, observe the number of residents in physical restraints and how frequently they are released. Restraints should be released at least every two hours or as ordered by the attending physician.

The issue is not whether restraints are used, but whether they are being used properly. You should always ask why restraints are used, how frequently they are released, and what the physician has ordered regarding their use. You need to feel reassured that restraints are used only for the physical safety of residents or to provide proper medical treatment and care.

Resident Adjustment Periods

The average adjustment time for residents entering a nursing home is six months. Obviously, this depends on an individual's overall attitude and/or health conditions. Family members can assist the resident in smoothing out the adjustment period by following some important steps.

Step 1—Take a positive stance toward the nursing home and express this. Remember, your loved one is moving into a new and strange environment, and he or she does not need other persons causing confusion and raising levels of anxiety about the admission. The move was necessary because health needs demanded the care offered by medical professionals and specialists in a nursing home.

Step 2—Follow the advice of the nursing staff about visitation. They often recommend that family members not visit for a period of two to three weeks after admission because this isolation helps them settle residents into their new environment.

Step 3—Give yourself and the resident sufficient time to adjust to the new environment. Do not rush the process, and risk unnecessary emotional episodes. New residents often ask to leave. Encourage and support your family member to stay because he or she will receive good care.

I have seen so many family members take residents out of a nursing home against medical advice because they could not deal with the difficult adjustment period. Such action impairs the recovery of the ill residents and often affects their health. Usually, the emotional stress of accepting nursing home placement causes these poor decisions.

For many family members, it is depressing to see a loved one in a nursing home environment. As a result, some family members hate to visit, even though they actually want to spend time with their loved one. For many family members, their adjustment period is longer than the resident's! The feelings of depression subside in time, especially as family observes the resident's recovery.

Quality of Food

Food served in a nursing home is supervised by a registered dietitian. Meals are planned in seasonal cycles that include varieties of food generally well-liked in the geographic area of the facility.

Nursing home food tends to be more bland than your normal home cooking. Seasoning is minimum because residents need therapeutic or restrictive diets, and institutional cooking requires different methods of preparing food. Still, it is common to receive complaints about the taste of food, even though meals may be nutritious, tasty, and attractive. Additionally, remember the number of taste buds decrease with age, reducing the taste of and the appetite for food.

Possibility of Discharge

The most common misconception about nursing homes is that once admitted, the resident will never be discharged alive. This is far from the truth. As noted in Chapter 9, 75 percent of all nursing home admissions are discharged alive, and only 25 percent of nursing home residents die there. Most residents placed in a nursing home come with discharge potential once they recover from an illness requiring rehabilitative care.

Discuss your discharge potential or that of your family member with the nursing staff. They can give you periodic updates on discharge potential. The goal of all nursing care plans is an individual's recovery and/or improvement.

What You See Is Not Always What You Get

When visiting nursing homes, your observations are not always consistent with what the environment reflects on a 24-hour basis. The big question is: What do you consistently see and smell? Many residents are incontinent with no control over their bowels and bladder, but they are in an individual retraining program or period and usually in varying stages of the rehabilitative process. Excellent nursing homes attend to the residents quickly and have housekeeping departments that work hard to minimize offensive odors. Family members can arrive for a visit and find the resident in need of cleaning because the "accident" just happened. Again, the real question is: Do you consistently find the resident in that condition?

Consistency is the key word! Is the staff consistently friendly, caring, and courteous? Is the facility generally free from offensive odors? Does the facility typically give good patient care? Is the facility sufficiently staffed to care for the number of current residents?

Loss of Personal Items

Generally, it is desirable to keep a minimum amount of personal items, such as clothing, purses, wallets, rings, and money. These items can be registered with the facility at the time of admission for safekeeping. However, it is always better to store them away from the facility.

Clothing should always be marked with the resident's name and checked often because the name comes off with repeated washings.

Residents often misplace items but believe these items were stolen. Most misplaced items are recovered, many being found in the laundry or by the housekeeping staff after a period of time.

Fee Structures

A common misconception is that room and board fees cover all supplies and services in the nursing home. Generally, room and board include the room, meals, housekeeping, nonpersonal laundry, activities, and daily personal care. Additional fees are often charged for the beauty shop, personal laundry, nursing supplies, pharmacy, physical therapy, speech therapy, occupational therapy, meals for residents' visitors, and other individual services.

Usually, the room and board fee is billed one month in advance, while miscellaneous charges are billed retroactively for the previous month as they are incurred.

Residents' Rights Versus Family Wants

Occasionally, conflicts erupt over what the family wants for the resident and the requirements placed on the nursing home by licensing agencies to adhere to policies protecting residents' rights. There may even be conflicts between family wants and the best medical treatment and care for the resident.

Residents' rights, covered in Chapter 14, deal primarily with the protection of residents' privacy, preservation of their dignity, confidentiality, and rights having to do with medical treatment and care.

Remember, the facility must follow strict guidelines that affect all the residents. If there appears to be a conflict, contact the director of nursing services or the administrator to resolve the problem. Nursing homes are service organizations that deliver quality care under some strict, restrictive guidelines. Most conflicts between them and family members can be worked out through open communication with the facility's administrative staff.

Physician Involvement

Many people believe a physician is in the nursing home at all times as at a hospital. This is not true. All residents must be admitted by a physician's order. The specific care is determined by the physician and is supervised by licensed nurses, and it is administered by both licensed and nonlicensed staff. Physicians are required to visit the resident at different intervals every 30, 60, or 90 days—depending upon the level of care the resident receives. However, a physician is always on call for emergency situations in nursing homes.

Problem-Solving Steps

Once a person enters a nursing home, annoying or upsetting things will still happen. When problems arise, there are a number of steps a resident or family member can take. Begin with the easiest and the least confrontational step. If the problem persists, additional steps may be necessary.

Start by discussing your concerns directly with one of the staff persons involved. If you do not get satisfaction from that person, approach his or her supervisor. The following hierarchy lists the order in which individuals should be contacted if a problem persists.

- Head nurse on the resident's unit, who may be called the charge nurse

- Director of nursing services

- Nursing home administrator

- Ombudsman, an advocate responsible for investigating and resolving complaints made by, or on behalf of, nursing home residents

- State licensing and certification office for nursing homes that regulates the quality of care in nursing homes

Many things can cause a problem. Sometimes conflicts arise when residents and family members don't understand the nature of and restrictions on nursing home care. Other problems crop up when a facility error occurs. Regardless of the source of any problem, it is best to have an open mind while problem solving and to use the least confrontational approach that will resolve the problem. You will find that most problems are easily solved with proper communication between all parties.

Summary

It is common to set high expectations for the care and treatment of an individual you dearly love. Because your mother, father, sister, brother, grandparent, or friend is very important to you, naturally, the type of care and treatment they receive is significant.

Attempt to match your feelings and expectations to the capabilities and restrictions of the nursing home as it attempts to provide the highest quality care every resident deserves.

Understanding these common expectations and misconceptions smooths your part in the nursing care process and helps you decide about nursing home placement.

CHAPTER 11
CHOOSING LONG-TERM CARE INSURANCE

Long-term care provides you needed help if you cannot care for yourself because of a prolonged illness or disability. It can range from help with daily activities at home, such as bathing and dressing, to skilled nursing care in a nursing home.

Long-term care is provided by home care agencies, senior adult centers, adult day care centers, traditional nursing homes, and continuing care retirement communities. Family members often provide long-term care as well.

Definition of Long-Term Care

Long-term care refers to medical and supportive services for individuals who lack the capacity for self-care due to chronic illnesses or conditions requiring an extended period of care.

As you begin to plan for long-term care needs, you will hear references to the following various types of care.

Skilled nursing care is provided by medical personnel, such as registered nurses or professional therapists, trained for certain health problems or conditions. This care is available 24 hours a day, is ordered by a physician, and involves a treatment and care plan. Some people need skilled nursing care for a short time after an acute illness. Others require such care for longer periods of time. Sometimes skilled care is provided in the home with help from a visiting nurse through a home health care agency.

Intermediate nursing care is needed for persons in stable condition who require daily, but not 24-hour, nursing supervision. Such care is ordered by a physician and supervised by registered nurses. Intermediate care is less specialized than skilled nursing care and often involves more personal than medical care. Intermediate care is generally needed for longer periods of time.

Personal care assists a person with daily living tasks such as bathing, eating, dressing, and other routine activities. Its providers usually do not need medical skills. It is less intensive or complicated than skilled or intermediate care and can be provided in many settings, including nursing homes, adult day care centers, or at home. Sometimes personal care is called custodial care.

An Overview of the Need

The following statistics indicate the need to purchase some form of long-term care insurance:

- Forty-three percent of all Americans who turn 65 years of age will enter a nursing home during their lifetime.

- The average life expectancy of Alzheimer's patients is 12 years.

- Only 16 percent of Americans can afford long-term care.

- Nursing homes have 1.3 million residents.

- Approximately 7.5 million people receive some type of care at home.

- Every year one million persons go broke paying for long-term care in nursing homes.

- Two-thirds of all single persons are impoverished after one year in a nursing home.

- Among those who live to age 65, approximately one in three will spend three months or more in a nursing home; one in four will spend one year or more in a nursing home; and only one in eleven will spend five years or more in a nursing home.

- The likelihood of nursing home care is greater for women than men.

- The risk of nursing home care also increases with age.

How Much Does Long-Term Care Cost?

Long-term care can be very expensive, depending on the amount and type of care needed and the place it is provided. As of this writing, the cost of a year in a nursing home averages $30,000 and can be even higher, depending on various miscellaneous and specialized needs.

If you receive skilled nursing care in your home by a nurse three times a week for two hours a visit the entire year, your bill would come to about $12,500. Personal care in your home from a home health aide three times a week for a year, with each visit lasting two hours, would be about $8,500.

It is always advisable to secure the appropriate level of care at the lowest cost possible. Be sure to look at all your alternatives before making your decision.

Who Pays for Long-Term Care?

Normally, more than half of all nursing home expenses are paid out-of-pocket by individuals and their families. This summary details who pays the cost of long-term care:

- Private insurance   1%
- Medicare   2%
- Medicaid   45%
- Residents and/or their families   52%

Less than 50 percent of all nursing homes are Medicare certified, which means the majority of homes do not accept Medicare patients.

Medicare covers some skilled nursing care in approved nursing homes or in your home, but only in certain situations. Medicare does not cover intermediate or personal care or prolonged home health care.

Medicare supplemental insurance is private insurance designed to pay for some of the gaps in Medicare coverage, such as hospital deductibles and excess physician charges. These policies do not cover long-term care expenses.

Medicare pays for only certified, skilled nursing care, generally as shown on the following chart:

- First 20 days   100%
- 21 - 100 days   Co-payment made after $84.50/day out-of-pocket expense
- Over 100 days   No payment made

Further, Medicare defines skilled by services received and not by the type of illness. Other criteria include: 1) patient must have had three days of hospitalization, and 2) be admitted to a nursing home within 14 days after discharge from a hospital. The average number of days people qualify for Medicare skilled nursing services is 30 days.

Medicaid pays for almost half of all nursing home care. To receive Medicaid assistance, you must meet federal poverty guidelines for income and assets, and you may have to "spend down," meaning use up most of your assets on health care. Some assets, such as your home, are not included when determining Medicaid eligibility. When you have spent down your assets, you may then be eligible for Medicaid. Many people who begin paying for nursing home care out of their own pockets spend down their financial resources until they become eligible for Medicaid. Then, they turn to Medicaid to pay part or all of their nursing home expenses.

State laws differ about how much money and how many assets you are allowed to keep once you become eligible for Medicaid. Contact your state's Medicaid office, Area Agency on Aging, Department of Social Services, or local Social Security office to learn more about the rules in your state.

Should You Buy Long-Term Care Insurance?

Since over 50 percent of all costs for nursing home care are paid out-of-pocket, individuals are either spending their parents' assets or their children's assets. The solution to this problem—be rich, be poor, or be insured!

Not everyone should buy a long-term care insurance policy. For some, such a policy is an affordable and attractive form of insurance. For others, the cost is too great, and the benefits they can afford are too little.

Buying a long-term care policy should not cause financial hardship and make you forego meeting other more pressing financial needs. Each person must carefully examine his or her needs and resources to decide whether long-term care insurance is appropriate. It is also good to discuss such a purchase with other family members.

People with over $50,000 of assets, excluding their home and car, should consider long-term care insurance.

People with less than $50,000 in assets, excluding their home and car, will qualify for Medicaid quickly and probably do not need long-term care insurance.

The need for long-term care occurs gradually as a person requires more and more assistance with daily living. Or the need can surface suddenly following a major illness, such as a stroke or a heart attack.

Some people who have acute illnesses may need nursing home care for only short periods. Others may need it for many months or even years. It is difficult to predict who will need long-term care and for what amount of time.

Assess your odds of needing long-term care insurance coverage, take a hard look at the reasons you want a policy, and determine your ability to pay for it.

Whether you buy a policy will depend on your age, health status, overall retirement objectives, and income. For instance, if your only source of income is a minimum Social Security benefit or Supplemental Security Income (SSI), you should not purchase a policy. Also, if you have trouble stretching your income to meet other financial obligations, such as paying for utilities, food, and medicine, you should not purchase a policy.

If you have existing health problems likely to result in the need for long-term care—Alzheimer's or Parkinson's disease, for example—you will probably not be able to buy a policy.

On the other hand, people with significant assets may wish to buy a long-term care policy to protect these assets for family members.

Many people buy a policy because they want to maintain their independence and not burden their children with nursing home bills. However, it makes no sense to buy a policy if you cannot afford the premiums.

Insurance Shopping Tips

The following tips will guide you when shopping for long-term care insurance:

1. *Check with several companies and agents.* It is wise to contact several companies and agents before you buy. Be sure to compare benefits, the types of facilities you must use to receive coverage, the limitations of coverage, the exclusions, and the premiums. Policies that provide identical coverage and benefits do not necessarily cost the same.

2. *Take your time and compare outlines of coverage.* Never let anyone pressure or scare you into making a quick decision. Don't buy a policy the first time an agent comes calling. Ask the agent to give you an outline of coverage; it summarizes the policy's benefits and highlights its important features. Compare outlines of coverage for several policies.

Most states require agents to leave an outline of coverage at the time they initially contact you. If they do not give you an outline or tell you they will provide it later, do not deal with them.

3. *Understand the policies.* Make sure you know what the policy covers and what it does not. If you have any questions, ask the agent or call the insurance company's home office before you buy.

If the agent gives you answers that are vague or differ from information in the company brochure, or if you have doubts about the policy, tell the agent you will get back to him or her later, then don't hesitate to call or write the company and ask your questions. Beware of an agent who claims the policy can be offered only once.

Discuss the policy with a friend or relative. You may also want to contact your state's insurance department or licensure counseling program if it has one.

The final section of this chapter spells out many details in long-term care policies and will help you make an informed choice.

4. *Don't be misled by advertising.* Don't be led astray by the endorsements of celebrities. Most of these people are professional actors paid to advertise. They are not insurance experts.

Neither Medicare nor any other federal agency endorses or sells long-term care policies. Be skeptical of any advertising that suggests the federal government is involved with this type of insurance.

Be wary of cards received in the mail that look as if they were sent by the federal government. They may have been sent by insurance companies or agents trying to find potential buyers. Be skeptical if you are asked questions over the phone about Medicare or your insurance. Any information you give may be sold to insurance agents who will call you or come to your home.

5. *Don't buy multiple policies.* It is not necessary to purchase several policies to get enough coverage. One good policy is enough!

6. *Don't be misled by agents who say your medical history is not important.* Disclosing your medical history is highly important. Make sure you fill out the application completely and accurately. If an agent completes the application for you, don't sign it unless you read it, and make sure all the medical information is correct. If information about your health status is wrong, and the company relies on it in granting coverage, the company can later refuse to pay your claims or even cancel your policy.

7. *Read the application to insure it provides the coverage you desire.* Reread the application before you sign. It becomes part of the policy. If it is not filled out correctly, notify the agent or insurance company immediately.

8. *Never pay an agent in cash.* Write a check and make it payable to the insurance company.

9. *Be sure to get the name, address, and telephone number of the agent and the company.* Obtain a local or toll-free number if available.

10. *Carefully check the new policy when it is issued to you.*

Reviewing Long-Term Care Insurance

The following details are important to review before purchasing when reviewing long-term care insurance policies:

1. Determine what the coverage requirements are for:

   • Levels of care;

   • Home health care;

   • Assisted living; and

   • Adult day care.

2. How long is the benefit period for which the policy will pay?

   • Accept nothing less than three years since two-thirds of all nursing home placements last that length of time.

3. How much will the policy pay?

   • Select a reimbursement amount based upon your income and assets.

   • Average cost per day is $75 - $100.

   • Should have an inflation rider.

4. How soon will benefits begin?

- Not over a 100-day waiting period.

- Do not pick policy that uses the hospital as a gatekeeper for its services; one-half of all nursing home admissions are not hospitalized first.

5. Are there any policy restrictions?

- Look for statements regarding any pre-existing conditions.

- Check the policy for waivers of conditions.

- Check for policy exclusions, such as accidental injury and workman's compensation.

6. Is there guaranteed renewal of policy with payment of premium?

7. How much do you expect to pay?

- Get a competitive policy, but not the highest or lowest cost policy.

- Seek one with reasonable cost, one you can afford.

- Policies are usually discounted for couples.

- The cost of policies is based on your age when you make the application:

A couple in their 40s pays $700 - $800 per year.

A couple in their 60s pays $1,200 - $1,500 per year.

A couple in their 70s pays $3,000 - $4,000 per year.

- The average age of a nursing home resident is 80 years.

8. Does health affect policy costs and eligibility?

- Typically, your health status does affect your policy costs and your eligibility for coverage.

9. What is the insurance company's strength?

- Should be rated A or A+ by:

Standard & Poors
(212) 208-1527; or

Weiss Research, Inc.
(800) 289-9222.

Exhibit 11 compares five of the better long-term care policies. All are guaranteed renewable, do cover Alzheimer's disease, are written to pay benefits for at least four years, and are available in most states.

Most Americans protect their assets by having medical, automobile, and home insurance. Why not protect yourself from the devastating loss of all your assets and savings if the need for long-term care insurance arises?

CHAPTER 12
SOURCES OF NURSING HOME PAYMENT

Nursing home care can be exceedingly expensive, depending upon the amount and type of care needed and on the setting in which it is provided. In 1994, the average yearly cost of care in a nursing home was $30,000. The cost can go higher, depending upon various miscellaneous and specialized services.

Statistics indicate only 16 percent of Americans can afford nursing home care, and over one million people go broke every year paying for nursing home care. Two-thirds of all single persons are impoverished after one year in a nursing home. These statistics are staggering when you think of how hard and long most people work to save for retirement and to build their financial assets.

Therefore, the sources of nursing home payment are indeed an important factor when deciding about nursing home placement.

There are basically four sources for nursing home payment:

• Medicare,

• Medicaid,

• Private insurance, and

• Personal, out-of-pocket resources.

Obviously, depleting your personal resources or savings account is the last and final option most people want to choose. Therefore, you must understand how to access these other financial resources for nursing home costs.

Medicare

Medicare is a federal program that provides some coverage for medical costs for people over 65 who are eligible for Social Security. It also covers some costs for people younger than 65 who suffer from chronic kidney disease or who are disabled.

Medicare is divided into two parts. Part A addresses hospital and post-hospital costs in a nursing home setting. Part B is a supplemental policy concerned with doctor bills, medical supplies, and outpatient services. Part B limits what it will cover and costs a monthly fee for participation or membership. Part A of Medicare is free. However, Parts A and B both include deductibles.

Medicare Part A insurance is available to individuals over 65 or individuals who have been disabled at least two years. Medicare provides funding for some skilled nursing care in approved or certified nursing homes. Remember, not all nursing homes choose to be certified for Medicare participation. Medicare does not cover intermediate or personal care in nursing homes. The following summarizes the available funding through Medicare for nursing home costs:

- First 20 days   100%

- 21 - 100 days   Co-pay after $84.50/day out-of-pocket expense

- Over 100 days   Nothing

After you have paid the co-payment of $84.50 per day towards your care, Medicare will pay the rest of your daily bill between the 21st and 100th days in a nursing home. After 100 days in a nursing home, Medicare stops all payment.

Skilled nursing care is determined by Medicare and by the services received and not by the type of illness. Other criteria include at least a three-day hospitalization and admission into a nursing home within 14 days after discharge from the hospital.

Contrary to popular belief, Medicare policies contribute little to nursing home costs. At best, Medicare is an interim funding source available to some senior adults in a nursing home setting. When nursing home stays are less than 100 days, the Medicare program does an acceptable job funding required nursing home care.

Be sure to check if the nursing home you choose for placement accepts Medicare. There is a growing trend for nursing homes not to accept Medicare funding. The reason is financial. Nursing homes have to write off the difference between their normal rates and the reimbursement rates the federal government contracts to pay for Medicare residents. In other words, nursing homes are discounting their rates to Medicare beneficiaries.

If you want to find out more about Medicare and your eligibility, contact your local Social Security office.

Medicaid

Medicaid provides assistance through the state and federal government for low income people, regardless of age. It is not an insurance policy, and coverage will vary from state to state. The elderly account for approximately 37 percent of all the services provided.

Medicaid is the primary payment source of nursing home stays. Over 50 percent of all nursing home care is funded by its programs in each state.

To receive Medicaid assistance, you must meet the federal poverty guidelines for income and assets. The poverty guidelines vary by state, and you may inquire about them at your state's Medicaid office, Department of Social Services, or public assistance office.

In order to qualify, you may have to "spend down" your savings and assets on health care. Some assets, such as your home, are not included when determining Medicaid eligibility. When you have spent down your assets, you may be eligible for Medicaid assistance. Many people, who begin paying for nursing home care out of their own pockets, spend down their financial resources until they become eligible for Medicaid.

State laws differ about how much money and how many assets you are allowed to keep once you become eligible for Medicaid. Once again, you should contact the appropriate office in your state about specific qualification requirements.

Medicaid can be a long-term payment source for nursing home care; however, you must meet the federal poverty guidelines for income and assets. Medicaid pays for multiple levels of nursing home care, either skilled, intermediate, or personal. But the recipient must qualify for the specific level of care being received.

Most nursing homes are certified to take Medicaid recipients. However, there are some that do not take them, so be sure to check with the facility you choose. As with the Medicare program, Medicaid discounts reimbursement to the nursing home from their normal rates. The facility contracts with the state Medicaid program for a daily reimbursement rate for each level of care provided, a rate significantly lower in most states than the rate nursing homes charge private pay residents. Many nursing homes prefer not to accept persons on Medicaid because of their lower rates.

Federal and state regulations governing the Medicaid program protect its recipients from some aspects of discrimination. However, Medicaid recipients often face discrimination in being admitted to nursing homes or in the services they receive there. Quality nursing homes do not discriminate.

One other source of payment also bears mentioning. The Veterans Administration covers services provided directly by their vast network of health facilities and programs administered in over 150 VA medical centers across the country. These services include:

- Nursing home care;

- Personal care and supervision in residential care facilities;

- Hospital-based home health care programs;

- Care for those living in VA facilities; and

- Aid to state-administered veterans' homes at all levels of care.

In some states, family members of veterans also are eligible for VA services. If you want further information about VA services and benefits, you should contact your local or state VA office.

Private Insurance as a Source of Payment

Private insurance is the best method to pay for nursing home care over an extended period of time. However, only about one percent of the nursing home population has or uses private insurance as a source of payment. The reason is simply because individuals rarely take the time to explore purchasing long-term care insurance or wait too late in life to purchase policies. Chapter 11 deals extensively with this subject.

Private insurance policies vary in the coverage they provide and must be carefully examined before purchase. A number include some type of nursing home benefit, but it is important to note specific features, such as a prior hospitalization requirement, whether there is coverage for custodial care, or whether custodial care is covered only after receiving skilled care. It is also important to look at the amount of benefits, the

length of time benefits are paid, waiting periods, exclusions, and other requirements.

To avoid spending your own or your parents' assets or your children's inheritance, you should strongly consider purchasing private insurance to cover the costs of long-term care. The cost of these policies is relatively modest if purchased before the age of 60.

Personal Resources

You or your relatives' ability to pay nursing home expenses out-of-pocket will play a major role in whether a home accepts you or your relative as a resident. Consequently, the amount of your personal resources—savings, income, value of real estate, insurance benefits—is an important factor. Since nursing home care is so costly, many people enter a home paying for their care with their own income and savings, but must apply for Medicaid once their savings have been depleted.

Personal resources are the worst payment sources for nursing home care. This choice represents poor financial planning, yet most people choose this option as their primary means of payment for nursing home care and services. Nobody expects to live in a nursing home! However, 43 percent of all Americans who turn 65 will enter a nursing home during their lifetime and 84 percent of all Americans cannot afford long-term care.

Do not wait to make your plans

for nursing home care until you are admitted into one. That is too late. While there are interim sources of payment through Medicare, there are only two methods that provide continuing payment for lengthy nursing home stays—Medicaid and private insurance. The average cost of $30,000 per year for nursing home care destroys most savings accounts quickly. Do not be one of these casualties. Plan and prepare for the possibility of nursing home care.

Summary

Although government programs and private insurance cover some health care costs for older people, the major burden of nursing home care costs must be borne by older people and their families with their own income and savings. Family support is still important for providing care and keeping down expenses.

The programs that do pay for nursing home care services vary in scope and comprehension from state to state, and sometimes even within the same state. Many include strict eligibility requirements, and local differences emerge in the availability of similar programs. Regardless of the services and type of nursing home care, the question remains: How do I keep the cost down while getting the services I need? If you think you might be eligible for one or more sources for nursing home payment, explore them further, using information in this chapter as a guide.

The solution for finding sources of payment for nursing home care is simple: Be poor enough to meet poverty guidelines for income; be insured by some private insurance company; have a very short stay in a nursing home; or be extremely rich!

CHAPTER 13
REHABILITATIVE SERVICES

Rehabilitative services are a comprehensive set of specialties to assure the maximum independence, productivity, and satisfaction possible for an individual. Rehabilitation specialists—including physical therapists, speech-language pathologists, and occupational therapists—work for the rehabilitation of a wide variety of people.

Rehabilitative services are often used for recovery from cerebral vascular accidents (strokes), Parkinson's disease, arthritis, amputations, cardiac disease, pulmonary disease, low back pain, Alzheimer's disease, hip fractures, and many common surgeries.

For the elderly, physical therapy, speech-language therapy, and occupational therapy are often the critical treatments that make the difference in determining whether a person will need retirement housing, assisted living, residential care, or nursing home care.

The rehabilitative services described in this chapter are available primarily through the following sources:

- Acute care hospitals;

- Nursing homes; or

- Home health agencies.

Rehabilitation Programs and Senior Adults

Assessing an individual's functional capabilities is the cornerstone of geriatric rehabilitation. The abilities to walk, speak, transfer from bed to chair or chair to toilet, and manage basic living activities on an independent basis often determine whether a person can live at home or needs a long-term care facility.

Functional capability is often defined by three distinct levels of activities of daily living (ADLs):

1. A basic ADL person manages such self-care activities as bathing, dressing, toileting, and eating.

2. Instrumental ADL persons also manage such things as using the telephone, driving, shopping, housekeeping, cooking, laundry,

managing money, and managing medications.

3. Mobility or complicated combination ADL persons are able to leave their residence and move from one location to another by using public transportation. Mobility is more complex because it seeks to measure different people's abilities to cope with their individual environments.

Categorizing older adults in these distinctive ADL levels has become the standard in most functional assessment tools.

The most common reason for the elderly losing their functional capabilities is inactivity or immobility. Their activity levels may be curtailed by an acute illness, injury, or chronic illness. Environmental barriers—such as bed rails, height of bed, physical restraints, inappropriate chairs, stairs, and no physical assistance available—are the major causes of immobility.

Older adults vary more than any other age group in their levels of functioning. In other words, chronological age is a poor indicator of physical or mental capabilities.

Access to Rehabilitative Services

All rehabilitative services provided by physical therapists, speech-language pathologists, and occupational therapists must be ordered by a licensed physician in the state where the service is being provided. Services are usually provided in acute-care hospitals, nursing homes, and by home health agencies. Services can be provided in a home environment or in an institutional environment.

A brief description of these major rehabilitative services follows. As you read them, if you feel you can benefit from any of them, contact your local physician or home health agency representative.

Physical Therapy

A physical therapist focuses on improving mobility, decreasing pain, and improving strength and endurance following a variety of diagnoses. The physical therapist's specialized treatments assist patients in regaining some or all of a prior level of functioning for maximum independence at home or in a long-term care setting.

Physical therapists are graduates of an accredited school of physical therapy with either a bachelor's or master's degree. The physical therapist has passed a national certification exam and is licensed in the state where he or she practices.

Physical therapist assistants are graduates of an accredited two-year program and assist the physical therapist with the rehabilitation program.

Speech-Language Pathology

The speech-language pathologist provides ongoing treatments that include screening, evaluation, and therapy for language, voice, articulation, and fluency disorders. Causes of speech and language disorders include stroke, head injury, environmental or behavioral influences, birth defects, neurological diseases and injuries, viral infections, and neuromuscular diseases.

In addition, most speech-language pathologists are experienced in treating dysphagia—swallowing disorders—a critical problem often overlooked in caring for the elderly.

Speech-language pathologists hold a master's or doctor's degree and are clinically certified by the American Speech-Language Hearing Association. Some are in the process of completing their clinical fellowship year.

Occupational Therapy

Occupational therapists provide services to individuals of all ages who have physical, developmental, emotional, and social difficulties. These folk need specialized assistance in learning skills to enable them to lead independent, productive, and satisfying lives.

When a patient is referred to occupational therapy, the therapist first assesses that individual's abilities to carry out necessary developmental, physical, social, and emotional functions that relate realistically to his or her prognosis. This assessment, an analysis of the individual's personal goals, and the demands of his or her environment are reviewed; these become the bases of an individualized treatment program.

During the course of treatment, the occupational therapist frequently reassesses the client's status and coordinates the occupational therapy program with that of other members of the rehabilitation team.

Occupational therapists are graduates of a baccalaureate program accredited by the American Medical Association and the American Occupation Therapy Association. They have passed a national certification examination to be a registered occupational therapist and have completed a supervised clinical internship.

Certified occupational therapy assistants are graduates of a two-year program accredited by the American Occupation Therapy Association and have also passed a national examination.

A wide range of rehabilitative services is available to meet the varying needs of the senior adult population in different care settings. Rehabilitation programs that improve functional capabilities have resulted in improving the quality of life for many elderly individuals.

Summary

The physical therapist, speech-language pathologist, and occupational therapist oversee a patient's status in a supportive and educational environment. They provide in-service training and on-going education to other members of the health care team and the patient's family to insure carry-over of rehabilitative treatment.

Rehabilitation programs are effective and should be strongly considered. All rehabilitative services must be ordered by a physician. Once again, if you feel that you or someone else could benefit from a comprehensive, individualized rehabilitation program, contact your physician or a home health agency for a possible referral.

CHAPTER 14
RESIDENTS' RIGHTS

Residents' rights are included in this book because I feel it is important for each prospective resident of a nursing home to know his or her "rights" before entering a long-term care facility.

Every nursing home is required to have a written statement of rights and responsibilities that governs the actions of staff members toward residents. States require this document as a part of the licensure and certification process. They also require that it be posted on a prominent bulletin board easily accessible for residents, family members, and visitors to view.

The most important question is: Does the facility put into action what their residents' rights state? When making decisions about which nursing home to choose, residents' rights become an important aspect to consider.

Residents' rights help ensure quality of care and quality of life for persons in long-term care facilities. These rights include:

• Legal rights—privileges and protection guaranteed under local, state, and federal laws;

• Human rights—respect for privacy and the considerate treatment necessary to preserve dignity; and

• Other special rights—rights having to do with medical treatment and other areas of life in a nursing home.

Residents of long-term care facilities enjoy the same rights as all people. The Constitution protects everyone. Residents still have the right to vote, own property, marry, and enjoy the same constitutional protections as other citizens. They have the right to a high standard of care and a right to a safe, secure, and comfortable environment. The facility may not limit or take away any of a resident's rights except in certain temporary emergency situations.

Residents' rights are protected by law. The federal government protects the rights of residents through the Constitution and other special laws, and sets standards for residents' care. Each state also sets standards for residents' rights and care. The state licenses long-term care facilities, administrators, and certain health care workers to help ensure the best care in nursing homes. In addition, local building, health, and fire codes help maintain safety and quality of care.

What Are Your Resident Rights?

1. Be informed of your rights and your responsibilities. Facility administrators must know you understand all your rights and responsibilities. Staff should review these rights with you and notify you in advance of any changes. They also should provide you with a written copy of their residents' rights

2. Exercise your rights. Staff should encourage and help you exercise your rights. The facility must have a system for handling complaints. You must be allowed to use it freely and to receive a prompt response.

3. Be told of available services. You must be told about all services available to you and their cost. You must also receive reasonable notices of any changes in charges or fees.

4. Make treatment decisions. As a legally competent adult, you have the right to accept or refuse medical treatment.

5. Prepare an advance medical directive. This document allows you to state how you want medical decisions made should you become physically or mentally unable to make them for yourself.

6. Be informed of your condition and treatment. You have a right to: 1) choose your own physician, 2) review and purchase copies of your medical records, 3) know your medical condition, 4) participate in planning your treatment, and 5) receive a written care plan.

7. Be transferred or discharged only for certain reasons. Acceptable reasons for discharge or transfer are: 1) your medical condition, 2) your welfare or the welfare of other residents, and 3) nonpayment of your bill (except for Medicare and Medicaid patients).

You must receive reasonable notice of transfer or discharge. If you need help finding other care or appealing the move, the staff must provide it.

8. Keep personal clothing and possessions. You may wear your own clothing and keep personal possessions within reasonable limits. The facility should provide you with private, secure storage space.

9. Have time alone with your spouse. You are allowed private visits with your spouse. If you are married to another resident, you may share a room.

10. Confidentiality of your records. Your medical records are available only to you and to staff members who are caring for you. Only those who have a legal concern in your personal affairs may have access to your financial and personal records.

11. Handle your own finances. You have control over your money. If you give money to the facility for safekeeping, they must follow strict rules for its accounting and investment. You may have access to your money during specified, reasonable hours.

12. Meet and communicate with anyone you wish. You can see, or refuse to see, any visitor. Your family may visit at any time. You may take part in any activity in or out of the facility. There should be private telephones and meeting areas for you to use. You must receive your mail unopened.

13. Free from abuse and unnecessary restraint. Abuse means any kind of physical, verbal, or mental mistreatment including threats or harassment. Restraint may be used only to protect the health and safety of residents, and then only when strict guidelines are met.

14. Treated as an individual. You should be allowed to make your own choices about daily living whenever possible. The staff must respect your privacy at all times, especially during medical exams and while you are bathing.

15. Free from having to perform chores. Staff should not expect you to work for the facility. If you choose to work, you have the right to receive payment. In some cases, certain kinds of work may be prescribed as part of treatment or therapy. Remember, it is your right to help plan this treatment.

Conclusions

Many states have their own residents' bill of rights that may guarantee additional rights. For example, a state may give residents the right to:

- Choose their own suppliers of drugs and equipment;

- Keep their own hours; and

- Have their bed held for a certain time if they must temporarily go to a hospital or some other facility.

Medicare and Medicaid patients have special rights protecting them against discrimination and other unfair treatment because they participate in Medicare and Medicaid. For more information about these programs, contact:

- The nearest Social Security office (for Medicare); and

- Your state or local welfare office (for Medicaid).

It is up to the resident of any long-term care facility to: 1) respect other residents' rights, 2) follow the facility's rules, and 3) give the facility accurate personal and medical information. Long-term care facilities also have resident councils that promote residents' rights. These are effective groups for influencing decisions at the facility. Council meetings occur frequently within facilities and can:

- Communicate and resolve grievances;

- Influence public policy within the community; and

- Promote involvement to plan special events and activities.

Careful attention to residents' rights results in quality care and quality living. As a resident, you should know your rights, insist on respect, and take action if you think your rights are not respected. It's not only your right; it's the law.

Personal Planning

Personal Planning

SECTION 4
ALTERNATIVE HEALTH CARE AND SERVICES

CHAPTER 15
HOME HEALTH CARE

Home health care is rapidly becoming the preferred method of providing health care to senior adults. By bringing health care services to people in their homes, hospitalization often is prevented and nursing home placement is delayed or avoided.

The reason for this preference is simple. Home health care vastly enhances an individual's quality of life. Home care services can be offered at costs well below those of institutional health care, an added incentive to use these services.

Home health care is quality, coordinated, comprehensive health care provided to a person at home by a multidisciplinary team of health care professionals. Home care can meet the health care needs of the young, the elderly, and the disabled who suffer from acute or chronic illnesses.

Home care services are available based on an individual's needs for care. An objective assessment, administered by a multidisciplinary health care team, determines the extent of those specific needs for care.

Typically the referral sources for home health are:

- Physician;

- Medical social worker;

- The patient or the patient's family; or

- Insurance case managers.

The referral source notifies the home care provider that a particular client needs the services it provides. The care provider then obtains a physician's order, arranges to provide the services, and begins the services to meet those needs.

Home care services include skilled nursing, occupational therapy, physical therapy, speech therapy, medical social services, physician care, nutritional or dietary services, home health aide services, respiratory therapy, intravenous therapy, help with drugs or medical appliances, and a variety of other services.

The care given and who provides it depend on a number of factors, including restrictions on what is covered by a given funding or financial source.

Generally, three types of agencies administer home health care:

- Governmental or public agencies;

- Nonprofit agencies; and

- Proprietary (for-profit) agencies.

As a result, the number and kinds of services provided by these agencies vary greatly. Not all services are reimbursable under government programs or insurance.

The sources of payment for home health care, as of 1992, were:

• Medicare	37.8 %
• Medicaid	24.7 %
• Personal out-of-pocket funds	31.4 %
• Private insurance	5.5 %
• Other	0.6 %

Requirements to qualify under the Medicare program are:

- Must be homebound;

- Must require skilled services such as nursing, speech therapy, or physical therapy;

- Must be under the care of a physician;

- Care must be furnished under a plan established and periodically reviewed by a physician;

- Services must be provided on a visiting basis at a residence;

- A physician must certify all the above requirements; and

- Necessity of medical treatment at home must be confirmed every two months.

Medicare coverages must stay within the following boundaries:

- Must include part-time or intermittent nursing care provided by or under the supervision of a registered nurse;

- Must be ordered by and included in a plan of treatment established by the physician for the patient;

- Services must be reasonable and necessary to the treatment of the illness or injury;

- Services can include physical, occupational, or speech therapy;

- Medical social services must be under the direction of a physician;

- Services can include part-time or intermittent services of home health aide; and

- Can include medical supplies and the use of medical appliances or devices that are under a home care plan.

Thus, Medicare home health benefits primarily provide skilled nursing services to homebound patients. They are not designed to cover services that assist individuals in remaining in the community or at home.

Because being homebound is a key to qualify for home health care services, Medicare accepts the following criteria as proof a person is homebound.

- Normal inability to leave the home

- Considerable and taxing effort to leave home

- Infrequent absences of short duration

- Absences for medical care or adult day care

- Outpatient therapy

- Occasional absences for personal services such as going to the barber or beauty shop

- Considerable or taxing effort taking a short walk

- Use of supportive devices

- Assistance of another person required

- Special transportation needed

- Confined due to psychiatric problems

The place of residence can be any dwelling—apartment, home of a relative, home of the aged, or an institution. An institution is not considered the patient's residence if its primary purpose is to provide inpatient diagnostic services, rehabilitative services, skilled nursing, or other related services.

Medicare Covered Home Care Services

Observation and assessment— Covers a minimum of three weeks when there is a reasonable potential for medical complications or development of a further acute episode.

Management and evaluation of patient care plan—Provides skilled nursing service when underlying conditions or complications require a registered nurse (R.N.) to ensure that essential, non-skilled care is effective.

Teaching and training—Provides instruction for such things as knowledge of medications, home exercise programs, or adapting learned techniques to the home environment to achieve optimal functioning.

Daily skilled nursing care—Covers daily skilled nursing care if, from the time care begins, it is known care is needed for a finite and predictable period of time.

Medical social services—Covers psychosocial assessment, obtaining community services, as well as counseling.

Administration of medications—Provides Vitamin B12 injections as specific therapy for: specific anemias, gastrointestinal disorders, and certain neuropathies. Also pays for insulin injections if the client is physically or mentally unable to self-inject insulin and there is no other person able or willing to inject the client. Such injections are considered a reasonable and necessary skilled nursing service.

Venipuncture (lab specimen collection)—Examples include prothrombin time, fasting blood sugars, and complete blood count.

Ostomy care—Covers teaching ostomy care and providing immediate post-operative care; application of appliances is not a covered service.

Tube feedings—Provides for tube replacement, adjustment, stabilization, suctioning, and teaching the proper care and use.

Catheters (suprapubic or urethral)—Pays for insertion of catheter and sterile irrigation with medications.

Rehabilitative services (physical, speech, occupational)—Coverage includes assessment, therapeutic exercise, gait training, range of motion testing; and designing, fabricating, and fitting orthotic and self-help devices.

Home care aide—Provides for personal care such as bathing, dressing, grooming, hair and nail care, oral hygiene, skin and foot care, feeding, assistance with toileting, assistance with ambulation and transfers, and simple dressing changes.

For those who are Medicaid eligible, there are fewer restrictions. A wider range of health and personal care services may be provided, if authorized by a physician.

Enacted in 1965, Medicaid enables states to provide medical assistance and rehabilitation to aged, blind, and disabled persons and to families with dependent children in need of health care. Federal law does not define the term "home health services." Medicaid differs from Medicare in that it does not require "skilled" care, and patients do not have to be homebound. Regulations specify, however, that the plan of care can be provided only with written authorization of a physician and that the plan of care must be reviewed every 60 days.

Advantage of Home Health Care

I have no doubt that home health care is the wave of the future. A public demand is growing for health care services that are available in the home. The reasons for this increasingly popular approach to health care are: 1) home is a more satisfying place for health care delivery; 2) advances in medical technology make these services more viable; and 3) they are cost effective.

An article written by Val J. Halamandaris for *CARING* Magazine (Oct. 1985) addresses 20 reasons for home care. I thought his comments were excellent and worth including in this book.

20 Reasons for Home Care

1. It is delivered at home. There are such positive feelings that all of us associate with being home. When we are not feeling well, most of us ask to go home. When we are feeling well, we enjoy the sanctity of our residences and the joy of being with our loved ones.

2. Home care represents the best tradition in American health care. Home health agencies were started as public agencies to seek out the poor and needy who otherwise would go without care. No one was turned away. This is still true for most of America's home health agencies.

3. Home care keeps families together. There is no more important social value. It is particularly important in time of illness.

4. Home care serves to keep the elderly in independence. None of us wants to be totally dependent and helpless. With some assistance, seniors can continue to function as viable members of society.

5. Home care prevents or postpones institutionalization. None of us wants to be placed in a nursing home unless this is the only place where we can obtain the 24-hour care we need.

6. Home care promotes healing. There is scientific evidence that patients heal more quickly at home.

7. Home care is safer. For all of its lifesaving potential, statistics show that a hospital can be a dangerous place. The risk of infection, for example, is high. It is not uncommon for patients to develop new

health problems as a result of being hospitalized. These risks are eliminated when care is given at home.

8. Home care allows a maximum amount of freedom for the individual. A hospital, of necessity, is a regimented, regulated environment. The same is true of a nursing home. Upon admission to either, an individual is required to surrender a significant portion of his rights in the name of the common good. Such sacrifices are not required at home.

9. Home care is a personalized care. Home care is tailored to the needs of each individual. It is delivered on a one-to-one basis.

10. Home care, by definition, involves the individual and the family in the care that is delivered. The patient and his family are taught to participate in their health care. They are taught how to get well and how to stay that way.

11. Home care reduces stress. Unlike most forms of health care, which can increase anxiety and stress, home care has the opposite effect.

12. Home care is the most effective form of health care. There is very high consumer satisfaction associated with care delivered in the home.

13. Home care is the most efficient form of health care. By bringing health services home, the patient does not generate room and board expenses. The patient and/or his family supply the food and tend to the individual's other needs. Technology has now developed to the point where almost any service which is available in a hospital can be offered at home.

14. Home care is given by special people. By and large, employees of home health agencies look at their work not as a job or profession, but as a calling. Home care workers are highly trained and seem to share a certain reverence for life.

15. Home care is the only way to reach some people. Home health care has its roots in the early 1900s when some method was needed to provide care for the flood of immigrants who populated our major cities. These individuals usually did not speak English, had little money, and did not understand American medicine. The same conditions exist now to some extent because of the new wave of

immigrants and the large number of homeless individuals who roam our streets.

16. There is little fraud and abuse associated with home care. Other parts of the health care delivery system have been riddled with fraud and charges of poor care. There have been few, if any, major scandals related to home care.

17. Home care improves the quality of life. Home care helps not only to add years to life, but life to years. People receiving home care get along better. It is a proven fact.

18. Home care is less expensive than other forms of care. The evidence is overwhelming that home care is less expensive than other forms of care. Home care costs only one-tenth as much as hospitalization and only one-fourth as much as nursing home placement to deal with comparable health problems.

19. Home care extends life. The U.S. General Accounting Office has established beyond doubt that those people receiving home care lived longer and enjoyed living.

20. Home care is the preferred form of care, even for individuals who are terminally ill. There is a growing public acceptance and demand for hospice care, which is home care for individuals who are terminally ill.

Reproduced by permission of the National Association for Home Care, from *CARING* Magazine, volume IV, no. 10 (October 1985).

Halamandaris makes a strong case for home care! Little wonder the public is demanding that home care be made more available.

Choosing Home Care Providers

There are several methods for finding home health care services within your area.

- Ask your physician to make recommendations.

- Check the yellow pages in your telephone directory under "Home Health Services."

- Check with your area's Information and Referral Service or Agency on Aging.

- Contact your state Association for Home Care.

After you locate the available home care providers in your area, shop wisely and find the correct provider for you—one that offers the correct services and one you and your family are comfortable with in your home.

Sometimes physicians attempt to direct their patients to a particular home health agency. Your physician may not always know the scope of your needs when referring you to an agency. Remember, the final choice is yours, not your physician's.

If you decide on a home care agency, ask these questions before signing a contract:

1. Is this agency licensed, certified, or accredited? If so, for what services and by what organization?

2. Does this agency have written policies or statements regarding services, costs, and payment procedures? If yes, ask for a copy. If no, consider another provider.

3. Does a representative from this agency come to your home, consult with you and your family, and prepare a plan for the services you will require? Are copies of this plan then given to the workers in the home?

4. Can this agency provide references? In some cases, due to patient confidentiality, references are not available. However, if they are, follow up on them.

5. What type of training does this agency require of their employees, such as aides or homemakers, who are not required to be licensed?

6. What are this agency's hours? If an emergency comes up, will you be able to reach someone there?

7. What are the fees? Are there any minimum fees? What are the payment arrangements?

8. Ask to tour their facility.

Home health care is a viable option to explore when medical services are required. Remember, it is your choice as to the agency to use. If you believe that you might benefit from home health care services, contact your doctor to discuss the possibility.

CHAPTER 16
HOSPICE CARE

Hospice is both a philosophy of care and an organized program of care, designed for terminally ill patients and their families. Only recently has it become a key part of the American health care delivery system, largely because of changing public and professional attitudes toward death and dying.

Hospice care was one of the first federally introduced programs of managed care in the country. The movement has grown to include 1,830 separately licensed hospice programs. Of these, approximately 1,100 programs are Medicare certified.

The underlying philosophy of hospice care is that death, when it comes, should be handled with dignity, neither meaninglessly postponed nor hastened. The major advocates of hospice care stress the importance of its comprehensive, wholistic approach.

Hospice is not appropriate for all terminally ill patients. The patient and family must have decided they no longer want a treatment regimen that focuses on curing the disease. Instead, having accepted the inevitability of death, they wish to receive palliative care—care that eases the effects of disease but does not cure it.

The goals of any hospice program are as follows:

- To ease the overall stress and burden of a traumatic life experience by sharing in and working with the expressed needs—physical, emotional and spiritual—of the patient and family.

- To aid the patient in the struggle to maintain independence and experience death with dignity.

- To minimize the painful and damaging effects of a family's grief.

These worthy goals are fostered by maximizing the amount of time spent in home care and outpatient programs, as opposed to inpatient care. Hospice is a home care program with back-up inpatient beds, because most dying patients derive great comfort being in familiar surroundings and close to the people who mean the most to them. Most hospice programs require that a family member or another individual be available to assist in the coordinating care for the patient.

Hospice inpatient care is needed primarily when the patient's symptoms are uncontrollable or when the primary caregiver needs a respite. The majority of patients remain at home until death; however, some must enter the inpatient unit several times during the final stages of illness.

Hospice Care Services

Hospice services are available 24 hours a day, 365 days a year. Generally, hospice care services mirror the Medicare hospice benefit. Individualized services allow family members to return to the mainstream of daily living faster and help prevent grief related illness.

The following are some of the varied hospice care services:

- Scheduling needed visits of a registered or licensed practitioner nurse, nursing assistant, counselor, chaplain, social worker, homemaker, physician, or other volunteers.

- Twenty-four-hour availability of all team members through a personalized on-call system.

- All medications, equipment and disposable supplies pertaining to the illness.

- Physical therapy, occupational therapy, speech therapy, and dietary consultants.

- Extensive counseling services.

- Crisis care offered around the clock when necessary.

- House calls by the hospice physician as approved by the attending physician.

- Volunteer services including companionship, friendly visiting, and running of errands.

- Bereavement care, which includes counseling for family members at least one year following the patient's death.

Hospice care addresses all four types of pain: physical, psychological, social, and spiritual. Regarding physical pain, the hospice concept assumes that the comfort of the patient is the primary aim. The staff's responsibility is to anticipate pain and administer the appropriate treatment before the pain occurs. Psychological pain is alleviated by helping patients deal with loss of control over their lives and reducing the stresses of the dying process. Hospice programs provide clergy and other counselors, trained to determine the nature of the patient's spiritual and social pain and to relieve these in the most effective manner possible.

The hospice concept looks upon the patient's family and friends as patients also. The family is made to feel that they have done all they can do. Then they are nurtured by being involved in the caring process, allowed to aid in whatever way they can. The family is also supported by the hospice in the grieving process that occurs both before and after death. The family is taught the process of grieving and the various forms that the grieving process may assume.

An important part of hospice care is bereavement follow-up. While the form differs among hospices, follow-up includes visits by hospice team members, group bereavement sessions, phone calls, notes, and other means of supportive communication.

Eligibility for Services

Any age person diagnosed with a terminal illness is eligible for hospice care. Terminal conditions do not just afflict the elderly; anyone is entitled to the support of a hospice team and their individualized approach to rendering that care.

We live in an age of dispersed families and lonely people. Hospice care advocates for all people with end-stage illnesses and insures that none of its patients faces death alone.

Prognosis

The Medicare hospice benefit defines terminal as having "less than six months of life." States vary in their definition of terminal. The national average length of stay in a hospice program is 64 days.

Location of Care

Most hospice programs offer both inpatient and in-home care. Eighty-five percent of all hospice patients receive care in their own homes. Home is defined as the patient's primary residence—a single family dwelling, apartment, mobile home, adult care home, foster home, assisted living arrangement, residential care setting, or nursing home.

Choosing a Hospice Care Provider

According to the article, "Hospice Care for the Terminally Ill: A Logical Compassionate and Cost Effective Choice for Case Managers" (*The Case Manager Magazine*, July, Aug., Sept. 1993):

In summary, hospice care has come of age for case managers. The use of hospice services under certain circumstances can provide both tangible and intangible benefits for the insured and the payor. When coordinating the care in the final stages of a terminal illness, every case manager should consider the appropriateness of accessing high-quality, low cost care through a hospice.

Case managers can access hospice programs through the National Hospice Organization (NHO) Hospice Helpline at (800) 658-8898 or the Hospice Association of America (HHA) at (202) 546-4759. After determining the availability of hospice care in the patient's location, case managers can further qualify a hospice program by asking:

1. Are you certified for Medicare certified? (If yes, regular surveying, compliance to federal standards, and quality assurance measures are required.)

2. Are there other hospices operating in your area? (If yes, who are they? Do your services differ from theirs? How?)

3. What are your basic services? (Check these against a list of minimal services and compare with other providers.)

4. Do you have specialty programs?

5. How frequently do your nurses visit?

6. Do you require the availability of a willing and capable caregiver?

7. Will you work with our case management program?

8. What are your rates? What does this rate include? Exclude? (Many hospices bill per diem rates, which are charged for each day the patient is on the hospice program from the date of admission to date of death/discharge; but some may bill per visit.)

9. What quality assurance measures do you use?

10. What is your patient/family satisfaction rate?

11. What are your hospital affiliations, if any, in the event inpatient care is needed?

Funding for Hospice Care

Hospice care is a rational alternative when you consider the high cost of health care today. Statistics indicate that 28 percent of all Medicare dollars are spent on the last year of a patient's life, and half of that money goes for the last two months of life!

When a patient receives hospice services from a Medicare certified hospice, Medicare Part A hospital insurance pays almost the entire cost. There are no deductibles or co-payments, except for limited cost sharing for outpatient drugs and inpatient respite care. Because hospice is recognized as a separate, distinct provider entity, Medicare reimbursement goes directly to the hospice on a per diem basis.

Medicaid coverage for hospice care became effective in 1986, and private health insurance coverage of hospice care has increased dramatically in the past few years.

Hospice care is cost effective. At the same time, hospice care allows the recipient and his or her family a high quality of care. Some known statistics regarding the cost effectiveness of hospice care are:

- Average savings of $1,500 per patient per hospital stay in the last 60 days of life.

- Reduced medication costs by $300 per month.

- Elimination of all other home care ancillary costs in the last 60 to 90 days of life.
- Elimination of unnecessary and costly emergency room visits in the last 60 days of life.

- Reduced nursing home days.

Summary

Hospice care is a viable alternative for hospital, nursing home, and other institutional health care settings and is cost effective in the delivery of health care. Because most hospice care is in the home, it is a good resource for caregivers.

CHAPTER 17
ALZHEIMER'S DISEASE CARE

Alzheimer's disease is a progressively degenerative disease that attacks the brain and impairs memory, thinking, and behavior. It affects four million American adults and is the most common form of dementia. More than 100,000 of its sufferers die each year, making it the fourth leading cause of death in adults after heart disease, cancer, and strokes.

First diagnosed by Dr. Alois Alzheimer in 1907, the disease knows no social or economic boundaries and affects men and women almost equally. Most victims are over 65, but the disease can strike people in their 40s and 50s. The problem is devastating for both victims and their families, and has been called the disease of the century. It eventually renders victims totally incapable of caring for themselves.

The cause of Alzheimer's disease is not known, although it is currently receiving intensive scientific investigation. Nor is there a single clinical test to identify it.

Alzheimer's is not a normal consequence of aging. It is an organic brain disease that afflicts about 10 percent of Americans by age 65. This means that 1 out of 10 persons at age 65 will have Alzheimer's. Of Americans 85 years of age, 1 out of 2 persons will have Alzheimer's. These statistics are staggering, and as the number of older Americans increases, so will Alzheimer's disease.

No two patients follow precisely the same course or progress at the same speed. The disease has a gradual onset. Symptoms include difficulty with memory and loss of intellectual abilities severe enough to interfere with routine work or social activities. The patient also experiences confusion, language problems, poor or decreased judgment, disorientation in place and time, and changes in behavior or personality. Eventually, the disease leaves its victims totally unable to care for themselves. The average time from diagnosis to death is eight years.

Caring for the Alzheimer's patient takes a professional, well-trained staff that understands the disease and is committed to improving the patient's quality of life. It requires working with family members to provide the support necessary to cope with the disease. And it requires uncluttered, well-organized environments with consistent routines. Most of all, it demands love.

I actually felt better once I knew what was wrong with my mother, even though I knew she would only get worse. At least I knew what I was dealing with. Before, I was scared and confused. I thought we were both going crazy.
— daughter of an
Alzheimer's patient

My wife refused to believe I was her husband. Every day we went through the same routine. I would tell her we had been married for 30 years and that we had four children. She listened, but she still thought she lived in her hometown with her parents. Every night when I got into bed, she'd say, "Who are you?"
— husband of an
Alzheimer's patient

Tragically, stories like these have become increasingly common with the speed of Alzheimer's disease.

One of my long-time friends recently visited Phoenix and told me about her son-in-law who was stricken with Alzheimer's disease. He has had the disease only two years, but already it has progressed to the point that he does not recognize his family. His behavior easily becomes agitated and aggressive, but his family remains patient and visits him daily.

What a sad situation, not only for this man, but also for his family who loves him. Moreover, the circumstances are so bleak because there is no cure.

I want to share some insights on the care and treatment of persons afflicted with Alzheimer's disease. The following guidelines are to assist you in locating facilities to care for victims of this dreaded disease.

Staffing

Day and evening shifts must have enough staff to insure customized, not assembly line, care. This is especially important on night shifts so that residents who are awake are supervised instead of medicating them to make them sleep.

Good facilities have a minimum of 3.0 nursing hours per patient per day. For example, if there are 20 patients in an Alzheimer's unit, there should be a minimum of 60 nursing hours scheduled each day. Sixty hours divided by 8 hours, a normal work day, equals 7.5 staff members per shift assigned to the Alzheimer's unit for care and treatment.

The Staff

Alzheimer's residents suffer physical illnesses with behavioral symptoms so those who provide medical and nursing care for them need special training to understand the behavior and emotions associated with this illness.

Always ask what type of training the employees have who care for Alzheimer's residents. This training should be ongoing, not only to increase skill levels, but to train new staff. In the health care field, there is a very high employee turnover rate. Therefore, good facilities have an excellent training program.

Staff Training

Residents with Alzheimer's disease need a stable staff that does not rotate on and off the unit. A good staff never talks down or ignores residents, but treats them with dignity, humor, affection, and respect. Consequently, staff members should receive ongoing training in the special needs of their residents.

In many states, nursing staff are certified to provide care and treatment for Alzheimer's patients. Ask if the staff of the facility are certified, and if not, whether their training is specifically related to Alzheimer's disease.

Medical Care

A qualified person with expertise in geriatric medicine should see residents frequently, review charts, and be available for consultation. A psychiatrist should monitor the use of psychoactive medications and participate in plans to control problem behaviors. Medications should never be used as a substitute for staff time.

As you walk through an Alzheimer's unit, observe the activeness of the residents. This provides a clue as to whether the staff uses medications unnecessarily.

Behavioral Management

One main objective in Alzheimer's care is to create an environment where difficult behaviors can be reduced or tolerated without restraints and, in most cases, without medications. Staff should work for an atmosphere where residents relax, feel less afraid, still do some activities successfully, enjoy a smile or laugh, and feel they belong.

Observe the general attitude of residents, their activity level, and mobility when visiting a facility.

Therapeutic Programs of Care

Activities are vital to Alzheimer's care. A healthy schedule includes programs during the day, at night, and on weekends. Good programs not only encourage family involvement, but also support remaining abilities, minimize failures, support dignity, and bring pleasure.

Look at the activities program designed for residents. There should be multiple daily activities that provide variety and simplicity.

Safety Standards

The program should realize the special safety needs of people with dementia while also allowing freedom, movement, and autonomy, not to mention staff flexibility. The care of those with Alzheimer's differs from the basic care mandated by federal and state government. There has to be a secure but nonthreatening environment.

Look for adequate areas to walk and wander without danger for the resident. Good programs have outdoor settings and day rooms for this purpose. Most important is that residents have a feeling of security and safety.

These guidelines for the care and treatment of Alzheimer's disease can be summarized in the following statements:

- Multidisciplinary care team;

- All staff receive Alzheimer's education and training;

- Services meet the physical, medical, mental, social, and spiritual needs of Alzheimer's victims;

- Personalized plans of care and activities; and

- Education and support for caregivers.

Facility characteristics to look for in a quality Alzheimer's program are:

- Trained staff;

- Family involvement;

- Secure building;

- Freedom to move;

- Safety features;

- Activity programs;

- Reputation;

- Outdoor access;

- Medical services;

- Private rooms;

- Cost; and

- Location.

Since Alzheimer's disease is a progressive, degenerative illness, the stages of the need for continuum of care vary with each person. Following is a summary of guidelines for care required in each stage.

Early Stage (home)

- Medical diagnosis and referral

- Caregiver education

- Support groups

Mid-Stage
(home and/or residential care)

- Geriatric assessment
- Home health care

- Adult day care

- Respite care

- Residential care

Late Stage (nursing home care)

- Personal care

- Intermediate care

- Skilled care

Alzheimer's Disease and the Caregiver

Traditionally, women assume the caregiving role. Statistically, the typical Alzheimer's caregiver is a 45- to 60-year-old female, usually the daughter or daughter-in-law of the person with the disease.

Although there is no typical caregiver scenario, every caregiver, during the course of the disease, will be faced with some issue or patient behavior requiring adjustments. These caregivers need assistance and it is available. The Alzheimer's Association has chapters in all 50 states with telephone helplines, support groups, educational information, and many other services.

The Greater Phoenix Chapter of the Alzheimer's Association, in their January/February 1993 publication, offers some practical helps and hints for around the house.

1. Make a list of medications, physicians, hospitals, and friends who can be trusted, and hide some spare money somewhere. If you get sick or stuck in weather or otherwise cannot get home, someone will find these invaluable.

2. Hide a spare key outside. Lots of patients accidentally lock the caregiver out of the house.

3. Put phone numbers for the doctor, ambulance, and police beside your telephone. When you need these numbers, you will have a hard time using a telephone book.

4. Move anything important out of sight.

5. Consider removing coffee tables and other such items from the living area. If the patient falls, noncushioned wood can inflict great damage.

6. Keep the environment constant. Do not move the furniture regularly. Never wax floors to such a degree that they become slippery. Consider removing throw rugs.

7. Stairs can be dangerous. Put childproof fences at their entrance and exit. You might consider a small ramp at the front door.

8. Consider painting the top and bottom steps of stairs a different color. Patients fall on these steps more often than all the rest.

9. Plastic or rubber covers for door knobs are available on the market that will make it difficult for the patient to leave the house unannounced.

10. Alarms that go off when you touch a door now can be purchased from RV dealers.

11. Contact your fire department. They often have stickers to identify rooms that have handicapped persons living in them.

12. A digital clock with large numbers is thought to be easier to understand.

Here are some sensible and practical suggestions from other caregivers:

- Take one day at a time, attackling each problem as it arises.

- Acknowledge your right to feel angry, and then do something constructive to control it.

- Find satisfaction where you can, but do not expect much from the patient.

- Maintain a sense of humor.

- Try to put yourself in the patient's shoes.

- Do not assume the patient does irritating things just to be mean.

- It helps to learn as much as you can about the disease and what you can reasonably expect the patient to be able to do.

- Arrange for time by yourself; do things that restore your spirits and your perspective on life.

- Take a vacation now and then, even if it is only for a few days.

In general, Alzheimer's patients do best in familiar, uncluttered, and well-organized environments, and with constant routines. Those giving care must keep in mind that people never outgrow their need for love and affection.

Professional counseling can be extremely helpful, especially in the early stages of caring for an Alzheimer's patient. It can aid caregivers in understanding their feelings and reactions to the patient's actions and words and in recognizing their limitations.

CHAPTER 18
CHRISTIAN CARE AS A MINISTRY

The basic or fundamental reason for Christian care is found in the life and ministry of Jesus Christ. During His earthly ministry, Jesus was constantly meeting physical, emotional, and spiritual needs. As He was healing the physical ailments of people, His approach was always wholistic—ministry to the total person.

One word describes the difference in Christian care, and that is *compassion*. In the Bible, compassion means "suffering together with." As Jesus looked at the people, He saw the hurts, the needs, the suffering, and "He (Jesus) was moved with compassion" (Matt. 9:36). Literally, Jesus suffered with them.

As Christians, we are called to be compassionate to all people, to look at human needs through the eyes of Jesus who sees their suffering. Our actions, thoughts, care, concern, interest, compassion, and love are reflections of Jesus Christ living through us. We are the only Jesus some people will ever see!

There is a distinction between secular care and Christian care. Christian care involves something beyond merely providing "hands on" care as a matter of routine. It involves service or servanthood from the perspective of Jesus Christ and involves the very heart and soul of the individual providing the care.

The retirement years should be the most enjoyable and productive time of life. However, for many senior adults, it is when decisions reach peak proportions because of the significance of the consequences. Decisions regarding retirement housing and health care are some of the most important ones senior adults ever make.

"Cast me not off in the time of old age; forsake me not when my strength faileth" (Ps. 71:9).

"For whosoever shall give you a cup of water to drink in my name, because ye belong to Christ, verily I say unto you, he shall not lose his reward" (Mark 9:41).

"For God is not unrighteous to forget your work and labour of love, which ye have shewed toward his name, in that ye have ministered to the saints, and do minister" (Heb. 6:10).

I believe Christian care has at least four distinctives:

- Christian leadership;

- Commitment to excellence;

- Professionalism with a heart; and

- Counseling, guidance, and support.

Christian Leadership

In any organization, the leadership establishes the mission, purpose, and philosophy by which the organization operates. The leadership charts a particular course that makes sure the organization achieves its goals and objectives and every operating decision is based on the achievement of those goals and objectives. In Christian organizations, ministry is the primary, overall mission and purpose.

The leadership of most Christian organizations works from a mission statement of their ministry. In the case of retirement centers, their mission is to provide quality housing and health care to senior adults within a Christian environment. Therefore, their philosophy is to establish a Christ-like organization built on Christian principles and through the staff who put these principles into action to create the Christian atmosphere.

In Christian facilities, leaders seek the guidance of God in every decision. They sincerely want to know His will. The leadership conduct the organization and ministry in a way they believe Jesus Christ would approve and in a manner that would please Him.

Commitment to Excellence

The word *excellence* is frequently used by organizations regarding their perception of the quality of their service. Unfortunately, the word is used so often that its meaning has diminished. Originally, the word *excellence* was defined as the quality of being valuable.

Excellence is also the standard by which people or programs are measured. We live in a society that measures or compares everything! Most people want to be considered the best at what they do and so compare their achievements with those of others. This is why one of life's most important standards is how others see us.

Christian organizations are committed to setting the standard of quality care and excellence in service to residents. Facilities are frequently measured and compared against other retirement centers by the state agency that licenses and certifies them. Each state conducts a survey or evaluation of each licensed facility on at least an annual basis. A good measure of the excellence in care being offered is this annual inspection report of the state licensure agency. These results are posted in each facility.

Other good measures of excellence in care are consistently full occupancy and the length of waiting lists for any facility. Senior adults themselves recognize excellence in facilities that serve them and their peers well.

Many facilities use the term *excellence*. The real question is, Are the staff members committed to excellence in all aspects of health care—meals, housing, programs, transportation, recreational activities, social services, and therapy? The concept of excellence should be evident in all aspects of the entire organization.

Professionalism with a Heart

Recently a friend of mine asked me an interesting question. He said, "Would you agree that all retirement centers employ highly trained staff?"

"Yes," I said, "they probably do."

"Then what makes the care in a Christian center different from other facilities?"

"That's easy," I replied. "Professionalism with a heart."

Staff members at Christian institutions are professionals in their respective fields—registered nurses, licensed practical nurses, certified nursing assistants, physical

therapists, dietitians, and pharmacists, to name a few. Each is specifically trained in those skills necessary to care for residents.

"Having a heart" means showing empathy, compassion, and love for the individuals under one's care. Their work is more than a job; it is a labor of love. It's a ministry through which each staff member shares God's love by words and actions while providing housing and health care to residents.

When my daughter, Laura, was much younger, she fell on the sidewalk in front of our house and cut her knee. My wife, Donna, rushed out, put her arms around her, and helped her back into the house. Laura was crying because she was scared and hurt. But as her mother began to wash the cut, bandage the knee, and dispense some hugs, Laura's tears stopped and her fears went away.

You see, there can be a big difference in the way you put on a bandage. You can place it on as a matter of routine, or you can do it while expressing love, compassion, and concern for the one who is hurt. The latter is professionalism with a heart, a love-in-action attitude that is demonstrated every day.

The love, care, compassion, empathy, emotion, and personal relationship displayed by the staff of Christian facilities while serving the needs of residents make their work such a success. Their primary mission is a labor of love to meet the needs of others.

Counseling, Guidance, and Support

Senior adults require much counseling, guidance, and support throughout their later years of life. My experience shows they will have three principal counseling needs.

1. Dealing with depression.

Senior adults can become depressed when they lose a spouse or friend or have no one to talk to or share with. They sometimes adopt a dismal outlook as they age and become more dependent on others. Being alone or adjusting to new living quarters can bring on depression, too. Various emotional issues such as memory loss, loss of respect from others, being unable to cope with and accept their age and physical conditions result in depression.

2. Dealing with anger.

Senior adults often experience feelings of anger because of a sense that God has abandoned them. They frequently ask such questions as: "Why doesn't God just take me?" "Why am I still alive?" "Doesn't God love me anymore?" Many experience a sense of anger and rejection because of a perceived abandonment by family and friends. We frequently hear senior adults say, "They promised they would take care of me or come and visit me."

3. Dealing with grief.

Older adults often grieve over many things—the loss of family members, friends, home, personal belongings, health, mobility, independence, and the need for caregiving. Change always results in the loss of something, and loss results in grief.

Christian care involves more than just meeting the physical needs of senior adults. It involves ministering to the total individual by providing counseling, guidance, and support at an important time of life. Most Christian retirement centers have chaplains who provide this much needed counseling, guidance, and support on a daily basis.

Summary

I am frequently asked what makes Arizona Baptist Retirement Centers different from other senior adult health organizations. It is not our facilities or amenities nor is it the special programs or qualified staff. All of these are important. But what makes the difference is the part of our operation we call "ministry."

Ministry is the care we provide from a Christian perspective. We offer housing and health care for senior adults in a loving, Christian environment, and that is what sets us apart from many other organizations.

A couple of weeks ago, one of our chaplains received the following letter that illustrates my point:

This letter is to thank each one of you for the excellent care given to my mother. As hard as it has been for me to have her in a nursing care facility, you have made the acceptance easier by your loving care.

Mom chose Baptist Village on her own three years ago, much to my protest, but I respected her wishes. She knew in her own way that she would need all three phases of care offered at your facility and wanted it that way.

I could not have asked for a better staff of nurses and caregivers. I even thank the cooks who personally prepared the food for her special diet at the end.

Thank you also for allowing her to stay on the same hall in the familiar surroundings she was used to and with residents who looked in on her. I always knew she was never alone there.

Also, thank you and your servant's heart for coming to California for Mom's service. We gained much strength from your being there.

We appreciate your ministry to her and your prayers, love, and concern. Also for the support and encouragement you gave us through this past year and especially the Thursday morning support group. May God richly bless your ministry.

This is caregiving in a Christian atmosphere. Ministry through Christian care is what sets us apart. Many facilities use the term *Christian* or are tied to a church or other religious organizations. However, there is a big difference between professing and possessing that quality of ministry.

As one of many Christian care providers, we have a tremendous ministry opportunity to change and save lives for Jesus Christ. It is amazing how God opens doors to share His love and to tell others about Christ while meeting housing and health care needs.

Statistics tell us that 1 out of every 50,000 come to know Jesus Christ as personal Savior and Lord after the age of 65. At Arizona Baptist Retirement Centers, over 70 persons have come to know Christ through this Christian ministry.

There are so many other retirement centers across the United States that provide a similar type of Christian care. Thousands of senior adults are continually ministered to by caring professionals in these places. Their lives are enriched by the dedicated Christians who faithfully serve them. They network to send out a faithful Christian witness.

In **Exhibit 12**, you will find a directory of Southern Baptist Related Housing and Health Care Facilities for the Aging. These facilities represent retirement communities and homes modeled after the compassionate ministry of Jesus Christ. I trust it will be a helpful resource for you or for someone you love.

Personal Planning

Personal Planning

Conclusion

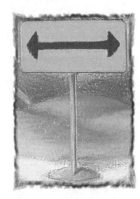

Confronting the situations that come with living longer is a challenge. Most of us would choose to maintain our independence and go on doing as many of the things we enjoy with the least number of restrictions. Making the right choice is never easy, but it is within our power to choose wisely. We owe it to ourselves and those around us to prepare now for the decisions ahead.

This book can be your guide to making the right decisions. It was written to assist senior adults and those who care about them to face one of their greatest challenges—the need to understand retirement housing and health care options and choose wisely among them.

These alternatives have been discussed in this book from a global standpoint. Some have been given greater coverage in the book because of the significant health risk, financial impact, and overall importance of making the right decision. To understand, analyze, and make rational decisions enables you to make the right choice at the right time.

Your ability to perform everyday activities is the key to determining your precise retirement housing and health care options. An assessment like the one found in Chapter 1 on a periodic basis will keep you aware of your abilities and any necessary adjustments you must consider.

Periodic reviews of this book will help you plan for the future or choose services that may be needed now by you, a friend, or a family member. Whoever it is, you or a loved one, active or confined, frail or disabled, this guide was designed to help you make the right decisions in an objective manner. Thus, your choices can be made with confidence, knowing that all alternatives have been reviewed and examined against detailed criteria. So the ultimate decision can be yours.

Personal Planning

EXHIBITS

EXHIBIT 1

SELECTED BIBLIOGRAPHY
The Family and Caregiving for the Elderly

Bear, Mary, "Social Networks and Health: Impact on Returning Home After Entry into Residential Care Home," *The Gerontologist*, Feb. 1990, pp. 30ff.

Beck, Melinda, "The Geezer Boom," *Newsweek Special Issue*, 1992, pp. 62ff.

Brody, Elaine M., Norah P. Dempsey, and Rachel A. Pruchno, "Mental Health of Sons and Daughters of the Institutionalized Aged," *The Gerontologist*, Apr. 1990, pp. 212ff.

Cantor, Marjorie H., "Family and Community: Changing Roles in an Aging Society," *The Gerontologist*, 1991, pp. 337ff.

Cattanach, Lynn and Jaco K. Tebes, "The Nature of Elder Impairment and Its Impact on Family Caregivers' Health and Psychosocial Functioning," *The Gerontologist*, Apr. 1991, pp. 246ff.

Goetting, Marsha A. and Vicki L. Schmall, "Talking with Aging Parents About Finances," *Journal of Home Economics*, Spring 1993, pp. 42ff.

Guberman, Nancy, Pierre Maheu, and Chantal Maille, "Women as Family Caregivers: Why Do They Care?" *The Gerontologist*, Oct. 1992, pp. 607ff.

High, Dallas M., "A New Myth About Families of Older People?" *The Gerontologist*, The Forum, 1991, pp. 611ff.

Huston, Patricia, "Family Care of the Elderly and Caregiver Stress," *American Family Physician*, Sept. 1990, pp. 671ff.

Johnson, Geneva B., "American Families: Changes and Challenges," *The Journal of Contemporary Human Services*, Oct. 1991, pp. 502ff.

Kain, Edward L., *The Myth of Family Decline*, (Lexington, Ken.: Lexington Press, Inc., 1990).

McCullough, Laurence, Nancy L. Wilson, Thomas A. Teasdale, Anna L. Kolpakchi, and Jerome R. Skelly, "Mapping Personal, Familial and Professional Values in Long-Term Care Decisions," *The Gerontologist*, June 1993, pp. 324ff.

Matthes, Karen, "A Coming of Age for Intergenerational Care," *HR Focus*, June 1993, pp. 10ff.

Meyer, Mardonna Harington, "Family Status and Poverty Among Older Women; The Gendered Distribution of Retirement Income in the United States," *Social Problems*, Nov. 1990, pp. 551ff.

Mullins, Larry C. and Elizabeth Dugan, "The Influence of Depression, and Family and Friendship Relations on Residents' Loneliness in Congregate Housing," *The Gerontologist*, June 1990, pp. 377ff.

Smith, Gregory C., Mary F. Smith, and Ronald W. Toseland, "Problems Identified by Family Caregivers in Counseling," *The Gerontologist*, Feb. 1991, pp. 15ff.

Silverstein, Merril and Eugene Litwak, "A Task-Specific Typology of Intergenerational Family Structure in Later Life," *The Gerontologist*, Apr. 1993, pp. 358ff.

Stevens, Ellen S., "Reciprocity In Social Support: An Advantage for the Aging Family," *Journal of Contemporary Human Services*, Nov. 1992, pp. 533ff.

Stone, Robyn, "Defining Family Caregiving of the Elderly: Implications for Research and Public Policy," *The Gerontologist*, Dec. 1991, pp. 724ff.

Tennstedt, Sharon L., Katherine M. Skinner, Lisa M. Sullivan, and John B. McKinlay, "Response Comparability of Family and Staff Proxies for Nursing Home Residents," *The American Journal of Public Health*, May 1992, pp. 747ff.

USA Today, "Aging Parents Drain Time and Money," Dec. 1991, pp. 11.

"We, the American Elderly," U.S. Department of Commerce, Economics and Statistics Administration, Bureau of the Census, September 1993.

Exhibit 2

LEASE AGREEMENT FOR INDEPENDENT LIVING

CONTENTS

LEASE AGREEMENT FOR INDEPENDENT LIVING

This Agreement is made and entered into this _____ day of _____,
19_____, by and between _____, as LESSEE, (hereinafter referred
to as "Resident(s)") and (*Name of Center*), (*Address of Center*), as LESSOR, (hereinafter
referred to as "Center").

ARTICLE I

SERVICES

Center agrees to furnish the services set forth on Exhibit "A" as long as Resident carries out
his obligations under this Agreement.

ARTICLE II

RENT AND FEES

A. <u>Rental</u>. Resident shall pay Center the sum of _____ Dollars
    ($_____) on the first day of each month. Center acknowledges receipt of
    _____ Dollars ($_____) representing the first
    month's rent. Rent may be adjusted from time to time (ad hoc) by Center at its
    discretion. If rent is not paid within seven (7) days after receipt of each billing, a late
    charge of Ten Dollars ($10.00) per day will be assessed.

B. <u>Tax on Rental</u>. In addition to and concurrently with each such monthly rental payment,
    Resident shall pay to Center all presently existing and future excise, sales, use or
    privilege taxes upon the said rental, or upon the receipt thereof by Center, which may be
    imposed by any governmental agency.

C. <u>Extra Charges</u>. Resident will be billed by Center for any services and supplies obtained
    for and furnished to Resident which are not provided for hereunder in return for the
    basic rent; and such bills shall be paid within seven (7) days after receipt.

ARTICLE III

SECURITY DEPOSIT

Resident has paid to Center the sum of _____ Dollars ($_____) as a refundable Security Deposit. Such deposit shall be held or applied by Center during the term of this Agreement to insure compliance by Resident with the provisions of this Agreement and (*Any state regulations*). Upon termination of this Agreement for any reason, Center shall have the right to retain or apply so much of this Security Deposit or advance rental as shall reimburse Center for damages suffered by Resident's failure to comply with this Agreement or (*Any state regulations*) and to pay to Center rental accrued at the time of termination.

ARTICLE IV

CHANGE OF ACCOMMODATIONS

A Resident's Unit may be reassigned under any one of the following conditions:

1. When the Resident(s) is (are) deceased;

2. When the Resident(s) gives (give) written notice of termination of residency;

3. When the Center terminates a Resident's occupancy; or

4. When the Resident(s) is (are), in the sole discretion of the Center, unable to care for his/her own needs.

ARTICLE V

TERMINATION

A. Termination by Resident. This Agreement may be terminated by Resident at any time by giving Center ninety (90) days written notice of his desire to do so. This Agreement may not be terminated in less than ninety (90) days except by mutual agreement of Center and Resident in writing; and until such termination Resident will continue to pay the established Monthly Fee together with such amounts as will cover other expenses incurred by or for Resident and any repairs to or replacement of the property of Center caused by Resident whether willfully or by neglect.

B. <u>Termination by Center</u>

1. Center reserves the right to cancel this Agreement without liability and with full refund of all payments made hereunder if there is a material deterioration of Resident's mental and/or physical condition prior to the date of his occupancy in Center.

2. Center reserves the right to dismiss Resident with or without good cause at any time after occupancy, in the sole discretion of Center. Center will give Resident thirty (30) days written notice. This Agreement may not be terminated in less than the thirty (30) days except by mutual agreement in writing by Center and Resident. Until the effective date of termination, Resident will continue to pay the established Monthly Fee together with such amounts as will cover other expenses incurred by or for Resident and any repairs to or replacement of the property of Center caused by Resident whether willfully or by neglect.

C. <u>Guarantee of Unit Retention</u>. A Resident who has transferred to a hospital for permanent care may indefinitely retain (his) (her) (their) Unit, provided the Rent continues to be current. A Resident who has relinquished (his) (her) (their) Unit will be offered a comparable unit, subject to availability, upon advice from Center's staff that Resident has recovered sufficiently to again maintain independent living.

D. <u>Termination by Death</u>. Death of Resident shall terminate this Agreement.

ARTICLE VI

<u>MISCELLANEOUS ITEMS</u>

A. <u>Representations</u>. All information furnished by Resident to Center in his/her application for admission to the Center is by this paragraph incorporated as a part of this Agreement and all statements and information thus supplied and supplied in this document are and shall be deemed to be true and accurate representations and warranties by Resident. Any material misstatement therein or any omission of material facts therefrom shall render this Agreement void at the option of the Center.

B. <u>Rules and Regulations</u>. Resident hereby agrees to abide by Center's Rules and Regulations which are incorporated as a part of this Agreement and such reasonable changes of or additions to such Rules and Regulations as may hereafter be adopted by Center.

C. <u>Center's Liability for Resident's Debts</u>. Center shall not be liable or responsible for any expense, debt or obligation of any kind incurred by Resident. Center is not obligated to provide any support, lodging or meals when Resident is absent from Center, nor any credit for absence from Center, except upon prior written approval of Center and in keeping with the terms of this Agreement and such regulations as Center may adopt.

D. <u>Non-Responsibility for Personal Property</u>. The Center shall not be responsible for the loss of any personal property of the Resident due to any cause. The Resident agrees to indemnify and hold harmless the Center for any injury to the person or property of the Center or of others resulting from the negligence of the Resident. Each Resident shall have personal liability insurance and shall maintain personal property insurance coverage. Proof of such coverage will be provided to the Administrator.

E. <u>Property Disposition Upon Transfer or Death</u>.

1. In the event of Resident's permanent transfer from his Unit to some other facility, all of Resident's property shall be removed within fifteen (15) days after notification by Center to Resident or his duly named representative.

2. In the event of Resident's death while still residing in Unit, his duly named representative shall have a fifteen (15) day period after notification, without accrual of the regular Monthly Fee, for removal of Resident's property from said Unit, after which ten (10) days if said property is not removed, the regular Monthly Fee shall again accrue and be payable until such property is removed.

3. If such property is not removed within the said periods of time by Resident's duly named representative, Center shall have the right to remove and store such property for thirty (30) days; and thereafter, if such property is not claimed, then title to such

property shall be vested in Center and it shall be disposed of as Center, in its sole discretion, deems proper, without any liability to Resident, his estate or heirs.

F. Resident's Liability for Damages. Resident hereby agrees to reimburse and hold harmless Center for any damages suffered or costs incurred by Center as a result of any act of Resident and/or his guest(s).

G. Center's Right to Entry.

1. Resident agrees hereby to give duly authorized employees or agents of Center entry into Resident's Unit at all reasonable times for maintenance and inspection purposes and at any time for emergency purposes.

2. The use of appliances in Resident's Unit will be prohibited without the approval of the Administrator.

H. Rights of Resident–Personal and Subordinate.

1. The rights of Resident under this Agreement shall not include any proprietary interest in the properties or assets of Center. The privileges and services provided Resident hereunder are personal and may not be sold or assigned nor shall they pass to heirs or personal representatives.

2. The rights and privileges granted to Resident by this Agreement do not include right, title or interest in any part of the personal property, land, buildings and improvements owned or administered by the Center. Resident's rights are primarily for services, with a contractual right of occupancy. Any rights, privileges or benefits under this Agreement or any interests or contractual rights of any nature in the Center are and shall be subordinate in priority, right, claim and interest to the lien, charge or security interest of any mortgage, deed of trust or security agreement now or hereafter placed on or affecting any of the Center or any interest in the real property or personal property of the Center, and to any amendment, modification, replacement, or refunding of any mortgage, deed of trust or security agreement. Resident agrees that upon request, Resident will execute and deliver any document which is required by the Center or by the holder of any such mortgage, deed of trust, or security agreement

to effect such subordination or to evidence the same.

I. Waivers. The failure of Center in any one or more instances to insist upon strict performance, observance or compliance by Resident with any of the terms or provision of this Agreement or its waiver of any such breach by Resident shall not be construed to be a waiver or relinquishment by Center of its right to insist upon strict compliance thereafter by Resident with all terms and conditions of this Agreement. It is understood that Center is not bound by any promises or representations made by its representatives or employees which are in any respect at variance with Center's Agreement with Resident as herein set forth.

J. Estate Provisions.

1. Resident agrees hereby to execute a valid will and henceforth to keep same current and to file evidence thereof in the administrative office of Center. Resident is also required to file in the same administrative office the name, relationship and address of his next of kin and/or the name and address of the person he wishes to handle his affairs upon his death and to keep such information current.

2. It is understood and agreed that Center is not responsible for Resident's funeral or other burial expenses. Resident is expected to make such arrangements prior to admission to Center or to designate some party to make them at his death and to file evidence of such arrangements in Center's administrative office.

K. Inability to Handle Personal Affairs. In the event Resident becomes unable to handle his personal or financial affairs and has made no other valid arrangement with regard to such circumstance (which is encouraged), Resident hereby requests any court of competent jurisdiction to appoint _____ as conservator and guardian of his person and/or property; or, in the event such named person is unwilling or unable to serve, then to name an alternate to such position in keeping with all the requirements of law.

L. Guests. Resident may welcome such visitors as he wishes for visits in his Unit upon such reasonable terms and conditions as Center may establish.

1. Overnight guests shall not be permitted without prior approval by the Administrator.

2. Resident shall be responsible for all meals and other costs incurred in connection with such guests.

3. No visitor who has any contagious illness or disease is permitted to visit in Center without prior approval from the Administrator.

4. Resident is responsible for any injury to others or damage to the property of others or of Center by his guest(s).

5. No one will be permitted to use Resident's Unit during Resident's absence from center without prior approval from the Administrator.

M. <u>Resident's Change of Units</u>. If Resident elects to move to another identical Unit to improve his/her Unit location, he/she will be billed a transfer charge to offset the redecorating expense of the vacated Unit. If Resident elects to move to a smaller, less expensive Unit, no Entrance Fee refund will be paid. However, if a larger, more expensive Unit is selected by Resident, an additional Entrance Fee will be charged equal to the difference between the Entrance Fee originally paid for the vacated Unit and the current Entrance Fee of the new Unit. In all cases, Resident's Monthly Fee will be the current fee applicable to the newly occupied Unit. Any moving expense will be the responsibility of Resident.

N. <u>Unit Alterations</u>. Resident may at (his) (her) (their) expense and with the approval of Center effect modifications of a minor nature to the Unit. However, structural, plumbing, electrical and mechanical alterations will not be authorized. Modifications which result in permanent installations such as shelving, drapery rods, etc. immediately become the property of Center and shall remain in the Unit upon being vacated by Resident.

O. <u>Binding Effects</u>. This Agreement and all rights and obligations hereunder shall be binding upon Center and Resident, their respective heirs, personal representative, successors and assignees and shall also specifically inure to the benefit of any mortgagee, assignee, or other lender of Center.

P. <u>Attorney's Fees</u>. In the event suit is brought (or arbitration instituted) or an attorney is retained by any party to this Agreement to enforce the terms of this Agreement or to collect any money due hereunder, or to collect money damages for breach hereof, the prevailing party shall be entitled to recover, in addition to any other remedy, reimbursement for reasonable attorneys' fees, court costs, costs of investigation and other related expenses incurred in connection therewith.

Q. <u>Notices</u>. Any notice to any party under this Agreement shall be in writing and shall be effective on the earlier of (i) the date when received by such party, or (ii) the date which is three (3) days after mailing (postage prepaid) by certified or registered mail, return receipt requested, to the party.

R. <u>Time</u>. Time is of the essence of this Agreement and each and every provision hereof. Any extension of time granted for the performance of any duty under this Agreement shall not be considered an extension of time for the performance of any other duty under this Agreement.

S. <u>Governing Law</u>. This Agreement shall be deemed to be made under, and shall be construed in accordance with and shall be governed by, the laws of the State of _____ and (subject to any provision in this Agreement providing for mandatory arbitration) suit to enforce any provision of this Agreement or to obtain any remedy with respect hereto may be brought in Superior Court, _____ County, (*State*), and for this purpose each party hereby expressly and irrevocably consents to the jurisdiction of said court.

T. <u>Construction</u>. The language in all parts of this Agreement shall in all cases be construed according to its fair meaning and not strictly for nor against any party. The neuter gender includes the masculine and feminine. It is mutually agreed that in the event any term, covenant or condition herein contained is held to be invalid or void by any court of competent jurisdiction, the invalidity of any such term, covenant or condition shall in no way affect any other term, covenant or condition herein contained.

U. <u>Severability</u>. If any provision of this Agreement is declared void or unenforceable, such provision shall be deemed severed from this Agreement; and the remaining portions of the Agreement shall remain in full force and effect.

V. <u>Additional Acts and Documents</u>. Each party hereto agrees to do all such things and take all such actions, and to make, execute and deliver such other documents and instruments as shall be reasonably requested to carry out the provisions, intent and purpose of this Agreement.

W. <u>Integration Clause; Oral Modification</u>. This Agreement represents the entire agreement of the parties with respect to the subject matter hereof, and all agreements entered into prior hereto are revoked and superseded by this Agreement, and no representations, warranties, inducements or oral agreements have been made by any of the parties except as expressly set forth herein, or in other contemporaneous written agreements. This Agreement may not be changed, modified or rescinded except in writing, signed by all parties hereto, and any attempt at oral modifications of this Agreement shall be void and of no effect.

X   <u>Captions</u> Captions and paragraph headings used herein are for convenience only and are not a part of this Agreement and shall not be deemed to limit or alter any provisions hereof and shall not be deemed relevant in construing this Agreement.

Y. <u>Indemnity</u>. Each party to this Agreement agrees to indemnify each other party, and hold it harmless, from and against all claims, damages, costs and expenses (including attorney's fees) attributable, directly or indirectly, to the breach by such indemnifying party of any obligation hereunder or the inaccuracy of any representation or warranty made by such indemnifying party herein or in any instrument delivered pursuant hereto or in connection with the transactions contemplated hereby.

IN WITNESS WHEREOF, the parties hereto have executed this Residence Agreement the day and year first above written.

_____	_____
"LESSOR"	"LESSEE"

(Facility Name) _____

a(n) *(State)* corporation, _____

By: _____   _____

Its: _____   _____

"Center"	"Residents"

EXHIBIT "A" To Lease Agreement

SERVICES

Center agrees to furnish the following services as long as Resident carries out his obligations under this Agreement:

A. Lodging. Living accommodations are provided in Unit(s) No. _____ (hereinafter called "Unit"), subject to removal and/or change only as hereinafter provided.

B. Utilities. The utilities (water, electricity and heating) will be furnished in connection with the occupancy of the lodging, subject, however, to the availability of such service to Center. Telephone service and television cable are the responsibility of individual Resident.

C. Furnishings. Within Units, Center will provide a stove, refrigerator, and garbage disposal. All other furnishings will be the responsibility of Resident subject to approval of Center. All furniture, equipment, appliances and furnishings and the installation and use thereof by Resident are under the supervision of Center, and the Administrator may require adjustments when the safety, health and best interest of all would be best served.

D. Board. Center may, at the request of Resident, provide Resident up to three (3) nutritionally well-balanced meals per day, served only in the dining room(s). Special diets will be provided only upon request of Resident and approval of Center. Any additional expense will be the responsibility of Resident.

E. Laundry. Any and all laundry may be done by Resident using the washers and dryers provided by Center. Items sent out to a laundry and all dry-cleaning will be at Resident's expense.

F. Other Services. Center will also provide the following services and conveniences:

1. Building and grounds maintenance and custodial service;

2. Scheduled transportation service;

3. Property taxes, if assessed;

4. Parking for Residents and guests;

5. Use of common areas and activities areas;

6. Fire detection system.

G. <u>Limitations and Expenses</u>. With a $300.00 non-refundable Pet Deposit, the Center will allow pets that meet the Pet Policy criteria. The Center also reserves the right of nominal supervision and, if necessary, may request changes in the furnishings, carpeting, appliances, etc., in a Resident's Unit when the health, safety and general interest of Residents are involved. All Residents are personally responsible to pay for sundries, personal effects, clothing, personal hygiene requirements, and food (other than meals provided under the Monthly Service Fee).

Exhibit 3

BUY-IN AGREEMENT FOR INDEPENDENT LIVING

THIS AGREEMENT is made at (*City, State*), this _____ day of _____, 199___, by and between (*Corporation or Facility Name*), a(n) (*State Name*) corporation, duly organized under the laws of the State of (*State Name*), hereinafter called the CENTERS and_____, hereinafter called RESIDENT(S).

RECITALS

1. CENTERS owns, operates and maintains a facility for retirement living consisting of houses, apartments, and a licensed nursing home located at (*Facility Address*), and known as (*Facility Name*), hereinafter called (*Name*). The (*Name*) is a community where retired people may live together in peace and harmony, with a spirit of cooperative good will, morality, and Christian neighborliness.

2. RESIDENTS have applied for residence in the (*Name*) and desire to occupy apartment #_____ at CENTERS, hereinafter called UNIT, subject to the terms, conditions and provisions of this Agreement covering such residence.

NOW, THEREFORE, the parties agree as follows:

I. ADMISSION

The UNIT is available to persons who are 55 years of age or older and who meet other qualifications for admission as defined by the CENTERS. RESIDENTS' birthdates are as follows:

RESIDENT _____, Age_____ (to nearest birthday)

CO-RESIDENT _____, Age_____ (to nearest birthday)

RESIDENT will submit a financial report, a current medical history, physician's report, and other documents and information that may be requested by CENTERS for CENTERS' review and approval prior to occupancy of UNIT. Approval is subject to CENTERS' discretion based on information provided by RESIDENT.

II. FACILITIES AND SERVICES

A. The following are provided at no additional cost to RESIDENT.

Utilities: Electricity, water, sewer, and garbage collection.

Maintenance: General maintenance including upkeep of building and grounds, custodial service in all public areas, and service on furnished appliances, repainting, cleaning of carpets, and repairs to UNIT as needed for the safety and well-being of RESIDENT.

Transportation: Scheduled transportation will be provided to shopping, medical and entertainment locations within boundaries shown in the New Resident Handbook.

Emergency Assistance: An emergency call system.

Activities: Recreational, social, and religious activities.

Mail: Private mail box.

Laundry: Washers and dryers.

B. The following are available at an additional cost to RESIDENT.

Telephone Service

Meal Service: Meals may be obtained at a daily or monthly rate. Apartment tray service is available for short periods of confinement at an additional cost.

Housekeeping

III. FEES

The fees for facilities and services provided pursuant to this Agreement shall be paid by RESIDENT in the following manner:

A. RESIDENT will pay to CENTERS the sum of $_____ as an Admission Fee.

B. The Admission Fee shall be allocated as follows:

1. The amount of $_____ of this fee will be a non-refundable "Development Fee."

2. $_____ of this fee will be deemed to be an "Endowment Fee" to be refunded to RESIDENT in accordance with the provision of (*Insert location of State statute*); and

3. The balance of the Admission Fee, $_____ shall be an "Equity Deposit" and shall be refundable to RESIDENT in accordance with the provisions of (*Insert location of State statute*).

C. In addition to the Admission Fee to be paid by RESIDENT, RESIDENT agrees to pay a service fee of $_____ per month in advance. Payment of the first monthly service fee shall begin seven (7) days after notice by CENTERS to RESIDENT that UNIT is ready for move-in by RESIDENT and shall be prorated to the first of the following month. The service fee shall thereafter be due and payable on the first day of each month. Notice to RESIDENT shall be given by ordinary mail. The seven (7) days shall be counted as seven (7) consecutive days commencing the day following mailing by ordinary mail of the notice of UNIT'S readiness for occupancy. CENTERS AND RESIDENT AGREE THAT THE MONTHLY SERVICE FEE MAY BE INCREASED BASED ON ECONOMIC NECESSITY IN THE SOLE DETERMINATION OF CENTERS. RESIDENT will be given thirty (30) days advance notice of any increase. It is understood and agreed that time is of the essence in this agreement, and that the monthly service fee must be paid when the same shall become due, or at such other time as CENTERS may, in its sole discretion, provide. Failure to pay the monthly service fee at the time the same shall become due, shall be grounds for termination of the Agreement by CENTERS.

D. Past due accounts shall be subject to a late charge of one and one-half percent (1-1/2%) of the unpaid balance per month until the account is paid, or as regulated by State law.

IV. RATE ADJUSTMENT OPTION

When a UNIT is occupied by more than one RESIDENT, one of whom dies, the survivor shall have the option of:

1. Retaining the same UNIT at no additional Admission Fee and paying a monthly service fee for single occupancy; or

2. Moving to a smaller UNIT (when available) and paying the monthly service fee for single occupancy of the smaller UNIT.

In no event, however, will any of the Admission Fee be refunded to surviving RESIDENT, other than in accordance with the provisions of this Agreement.

V. TERMINATION OF THIS AGREEMENT

A. Incidents of Voluntary Termination

1. RESIDENT may voluntarily terminate this Agreement by giving CENTERS sixty (60) days written notice of termination. In that event, CENTERS shall refund to RESIDENT a portion of the Endowment Fee and all of the Equity Deposit as provided in Section VI of this Agreement.

2. CENTERS may terminate this Agreement if the RESIDENT breaches this Agreement or proves to be incompatible with the way of life, or with other Residents of CENTERS. Termination for incompatibility shall be the result of a majority decision of the (*Name*) Advisory Committee of CENTERS. The RESIDENT shall have the right to present his or her views and opinions to the Committee before such a decision is executed. In this regard, after RESIDENT has been served with notice of termination for incompatibility, RESIDENT shall have ten (10) days within which to request a hearing before the Committee by serving notice of such request for hearing

as hereinafter provided. The hearing shall then be set and notice given of such hearing not less than ten (10) days prior to the date of such hearing.

The Committee shall advise the RESIDENT of its decision in writing. The parties in no way intend to waive or relinquish any other remedy at law or equity available to RESIDENT or CENTERS, including, but not limited to, eviction, forcible entry and detainer, or landlord's liens.

3. Failure of the RESIDENT to meet the obligations set forth in this Agreement shall be deemed a voluntary termination of the Agreement by RESIDENT.

B. Incidents of Involuntary Termination

1. Should RESIDENT die subsequent to the execution of this Agreement, CENTERS shall immediately terminate this Agreement and return to RESIDENT'S legal representative a portion of the Endowment Fee and all of the Equity Deposit as provided in Section VI of this Agreement.

2. Should RESIDENT become incapable of independent living and require care which (*Name*) does not, or may not by law or policy, provide in its independent living section, such required care and its cost shall be the sole obligation of RESIDENT, and such care is expressly excluded from the provisions of the Agreement. The right to make a determination of RESIDENT'S capabilities for independent living, together with the right to determine whether such condition and need for care is temporary or permanent in nature, shall be vested solely in CENTERS, after consultation with RESIDENT, RESIDENT'S physician, and RESIDENT'S immediate family.

RESIDENT waives any right of action against CENTERS and agrees to hold CENTERS harmless from any claims arising from its exercise of such independent judgment.

For purposes of this Section, the following shall apply:

a. **Temporary Condition**. If it is determined that RESIDENT'S physical or mental condition is temporary in nature, RESIDENT shall be expected to transfer to an appropriate facility or place to receive the care required for such condition. During this temporary period, this Agreement, including the right of RESIDENT to re-occupy RESIDENT'S UNIT upon termination of the temporary condition, will remain in effect. RESIDENT will continue payment of the monthly service fee.

b. **Permanent Condition.** If it is determined that RESIDENT'S physical or mental condition is permanent in nature, CENTERS shall notify RESIDENT, and anyone responsible for RESIDENT, in writing of such determination and its intention to terminate this Agreement, and RESIDENT will release UNIT to CENTERS. In that event, CENTERS shall refund to RESIDENT a portion of the Endowment Fee and all of the Equity Deposit as provided in Section VI of this Agreement. However, if RESIDENT transfers, on a permanent basis, to the Supervisory Care or the Long-Term Care facilities of (*Name*), the portion of the Endowment Fee and Equity Deposit otherwise payable to RESIDENT, shall be credited to RESIDENT'S account to pay for the cost of such care. **ANY COSTS OF SUCH CARE IN EXCESS OF THE AMOUNTS CREDITED SHALL BE DUE AND PAYABLE FROM RESIDENT.**

3. CENTERS shall notify RESIDENT at least thirty (30) days in advance of termination, except when a medical or psychiatric emergency or other situation arises which makes immediate transfer outside the facility necessary or desirable.

4. In the event of RESIDENT'S death, the next of kin, or RESIDENT'S representative, shall have a reasonable period of time to arrange for removal or disposition of property in RESIDENT'S UNIT. CENTERS shall have the right to remove and store all property from the UNIT for RESIDENT who is deceased or whose accommodations have been terminated. Property remaining after a ninety (90) day period will be considered abandoned and will be disposed of by CENTERS.

C. <u>Vacating Premises</u>

Immediately when any termination becomes effective, RESIDENT shall quietly and peaceably remove himself and his family and his property from the premises and surrender peaceably possession thereof to CENTERS. Upon termination of occupancy, RESIDENT shall quit and surrender the premises, equipment and furnishings therein in good order and repair, reasonable wear and tear expected. RESIDENT shall not be responsible for any defects existing at the time of the commencement of the residency providing written notice is given to CENTERS by RESIDENT of such defect within thirty (30) days after the date residency begins.

VI. REFUND FORMULA

Should this Agreement be terminated by either party as outlined in Section V above, CENTERS agrees to refund to RESIDENT, or RESIDENT'S legal representative, the following:

A. If RESIDENT withdraws or is dismissed from the UNIT within the first three (3) years of residency, the Endowment Fee shall be refundable in accordance with the schedule set forth on attached Exhibit "A" (not included in this exhibit) which is incorporated herein by reference. **AFTER THREE (3) YEARS RESIDENCY, THIS AGREEMENT MAY STILL BE TERMINATED AS PROVIDED HEREIN, BUT RESIDENT UNDERSTANDS AND AGREES THERE WILL BE NO REFUND OF ANY PART OF THE ENDOWMENT FEE.**

B. The equity Deposit remains the property of RESIDENT. When RESIDENT withdraws, is dismissed, or moves from the UNIT, or upon death of the RESIDENT (or remaining spouse), the Equity Deposit shall be paid to RESIDENT or his or her heirs at such time as RESIDENT'S UNIT is occupied by a successor Resident, but in no event, later than six (6) months following termination. There will be no interest paid by CENTERS on the RESIDENTS equity.

VII. RIGHTS AND RESPONSIBILITIES OF RESIDENT

A. This Agreement provides the right for residential occupancy under the terms and conditions contained herein. This Agreement shall not be construed as a lease, as a purchase agreement, or as a grant, conveyance, or transfer to RESIDENT of any right, title, or interest in real property.

B. The rights of RESIDENT under this Agreement are the rights and privileges herein expressly granted and do not include any proprietary interest in (*Name*) or the properties and assets of CENTERS or any membership in CENTERS.

C. The rights and privileges of RESIDENT under this Agreement to living accommodations, facilities, and services are personal to RESIDENT and cannot be transferred or assigned by act of RESIDENT, or by any proceeding at law or otherwise. No person, other than RESIDENT, may occupy the accommodations covered by this Agreement except with the approval of CENTERS.

D. Should RESIDENT desire to have an additional person live in the UNIT, whether a relative, through marriage, or otherwise, previous permission of CENTERS shall be necessary. The additional person shall have no rights or privileges pursuant to this Agreement, and upon the death or removal of RESIDENT from the UNIT, the additional person shall vacate the UNIT unless he or she leases or buys the UNIT from CENTERS at its then schedule of rates and charges.

E. Pursuant to the requirements of any bona fide lender, RESIDENT agrees that his or her rights under this Agreement shall at all times be subordinate and inferior to the rights of the lender under any encumbrance now or hereafter executed by CENTERS pertaining to the property of CENTERS, and RESIDENT further agrees to execute, acknowledge, and deliver such subordination agreement as such lender may require in order to establish the priority of such encumbrance as a lien against said property.

F. RESIDENT shall cooperate with CENTERS in keeping the property in good repair. Upon prior written approval of CENTERS, RESIDENT may have special painting and minor modifications, etc., done to UNIT at RESIDENT'S expense. Improvements to the premises made by RESIDENT in a permanent or semi-permanent manner, so as to become fixtures, shall become the property of CENTERS and shall remain on the premises when vacated by RESIDENT.

G. RESIDENT agrees to notify CENTERS of extended absences.

H. RESIDENT agrees to act in a manner which promotes the well-being and safety of others and to refrain from any act which may be detrimental to the facility or other Residents.

I. RESIDENT shall have priority over those on any waiting list from outside the (*Name*), for the use of other (*Name*) facilities as they become available and according to demonstrated need. Current charges shall apply.

J. RESIDENT agrees to be responsible for own medical care, to include but not be limited to, medical and pharmaceutical bills, ambulance and any hospital costs or fees that might arise as well as any nursing expenses incurred.

K. RESIDENT agrees that CENTERS shall have the right of access to the apartment by use of master key, or by reasonable force, if necessary, without any liability for damages, in order to inspect the apartment or to fix any plumbing, heating or other matter that may need attention. RESIDENT shall not change the locks or otherwise prevent CENTERS from such right of access. During the period after notice of termination has been given until RESIDENT vacates UNIT, CENTERS shall have the right to enter by means provided herein during the hours of 9:00 a.m. and 5:00 p.m. for the purpose of showing the premises to prospective new Residents.

L. RESIDENT agrees to abide by the rules and regulations for the governance of the (*Name*) and for the welfare and best interest of the Residents, and agrees to such amendments, modifications, and changes of these rules and regulations as may hereafter be established by the governing board of CENTERS.

M. RESIDENT shall not permit highly combustible material (e.g., gasoline) to be kept or left within the UNIT and shall take every precaution to prevent fire.

N. RESIDENT shall deposit garbage, rubbish and other waste in a manner and place prescribed by CENTERS.

O. RESIDENT shall be allowed to have pets in accordance with the established Pet Policy.

P. RESIDENT'S car may be parked on the premises only in areas designated by CENTERS. Boats, trailers, motor homes and such shall not be parked on the premises without prior approval of CENTERS.

Q. RESIDENT shall not pursue, operate or maintain any business on the premises.

R. RESIDENT may have guests on the premises, but no guests may stay more than fifteen

(15) days without the prior written approval of CENTERS. RESIDENT may not have overnight guests of the opposite sex without the prior written approval of CENTERS, provided, that such prior written approval of CENTERS for such overnight guests is not required for guests who are siblings (either whole or half), children (natural or step) or grandchildren.

VIII. RIGHTS AND RESPONSIBILITIES OF CENTERS

A. CENTERS is not liable for loss or damage by fire, theft, or other casualty, or injuries from the use of UNIT to RESIDENT, his or her family, or any invitee of RESIDENT. Any insurance necessary or desired by RESIDENT shall be at RESIDENT'S expense.

B. In case of injury to RESIDENT by a third party, CENTERS shall have the right of subrogation for all cost, expenses, and other obligations it incurs by reason of such injuries and shall have the right, but not the obligation, in the name of the RESIDENT, or otherwise, to take all necessary steps and procedures to enforce the payment of the same by the person responsible for said injury.

C. CENTERS reserves the right to charge a RESIDENT who damages or alters the UNIT, or other CENTERS' property, through neglect or conscious act. Damages may include, but are not limited to, the cost of restoring RESIDENT'S UNIT or other property to its original condition. CENTERS assumes no responsibility for any injury or illness resulting from such negligence or intentional misconduct.

D. CENTERS is an organization that is exempt from paying real estate and other taxes. Should CENTERS be required to pay such taxes in the future, a prorated portion of this cost will be passed on to RESIDENT.

E. CENTERS reserves the right to enter and inspect the UNIT at any reasonable hour, or at any time in case of emergency.

F. In case of damage to the apartment by fire not due to the negligence of RESIDENT, CENTERS shall cause the damage to be repaired. If the UNIT or other premises are destroyed or so damaged that CENTERS shall decide that it is inadvisable to repair same, this Agreement shall cease and terminate, and in such case, the Endowment Fee, the Equity Deposit and Monthly service Fee shall be adjusted at the discretion of CENTERS to the date when such fire or casualty occurred. The RESIDENT hereby releases CENTERS from any and all claims, except for its negligence, for any loss, damage or inconvenience arising from fire or other casualty, or, the termination of this Agreement, if such is deemed necessary in the sole discretion of CENTERS.

IX. ACKNOWLEDGMENTS

A. This Agreement constitutes the entire Agreement between CENTERS and RESIDENT. CENTERS is not liable for, nor bound in any manner by, any statements, representations, or promises made by any person representing or purporting to represent CENTERS, unless such statement, representations, or promises are set forth in this Agreement.

B. Where RESIDENT is two persons, those persons shall be deemed joint tenants with right of survivorship and not as tenants in common, and the term "RESIDENT" as used herein shall include both of them unless otherwise stated.

C. Where masculine adjectives or pronouns are used herein in referring to RESIDENT, they apply equally to the feminine.

D. This Agreement shall bind and inure to the benefit of the successors and assigns of CENTERS, and their heirs, executors, administrators, and assigns of RESIDENT.

E. This Agreement includes by reference the Application, Fee Schedule, as amended, and the Rules and Regulations (Resident Handbook) for Residents of the (*Name*).

F. If a portion of this Agreement shall be determined to be illegal or not in conformity with appropriate laws and regulations, it shall not invalidate or affect the validity of the remainder of this Agreement.

G. The failure of CENTERS in any one or more instances to insist upon the strict performance, observance or compliance by RESIDENT with any of the terms or provisions of this Agreement or its waiver of the breach by RESIDENT of any terms or provisions of this Agreement shall not be construed to be a waiver or relinquishment by

CENTERS of its right to insist upon strict compliance by RESIDENT with all of the terms and provisions of this Agreement.

H. Any notice required by this Agreement or bylaw to be served upon CENTERS shall be in writing and served by personal delivery at, or mailed to the office of CENTERS. Service of any notice required by this agreement to be made upon RESIDENT shall be in writing and deemed sufficient if delivered or mailed to RESIDENT at his or her UNIT. Any notice required to be personally served upon RESIDENT may be served by delivery either to the husband or wife or to one of the CO-RESIDENTS.

I. In the event litigation or arbitration is instituted to enforce this Agreement or in regard to any matter hereunder or pertaining to RESIDENT'S rights of occupancy, or resulting therefrom, RESIDENT shall be liable to CENTERS for all costs incurred, including a reasonable amount as and for attorney's fees if judgment or decision is rendered in favor of CENTERS, or in favor of the officer or governing board of said Corporation.

J. All application forms, medical reports, statements of financial condition, and other documents executed by RESIDENT or the agents, servants, employees or relatives of RESIDENTS, which are presented to CENTERS in connection with RESIDENT'S application, can be relied upon by CENTERS. CENTERS reserves the right to request additional information. CENTERS will not make public such documents without the prior approval of RESIDENT.

K. This Agreement is between parties and is not for publication or for the general public, and therefore shall not be recorded in the Public Records of any government agency, either in the State of _____, or in any other state.

L. This Agreement shall be construed under the laws of the State of _____.

Dated at (*City, State*) the day and year first above written.

FACILITY NAME

BY _____

Its _____

ATTEST:

_____   _____
Attest   RESIDENT

_____   _____
Attest   RESIDENT

(*Name*) provides services to qualified individuals without regard to race, color, sex, national origin, religion, or disability.

Exhibit 4

LIFE TENANCY AGREEMENT FOR INDEPENDENT LIVING

This Agreement is made and entered into this _____ day of _____, 199____, by and between (Tenant), (hereinafter referred to as "RESIDENT(S)") and (Facility Name and Address) (hereinafter referred to as "CENTER").

ARTICLE I

LIFE TENANCY PROVISIONS

The parties hereto have executed a Life Tenancy Agreement whereby (RESIDENT/RESIDENTS) have the right to reside in the Unit for their lifetimes. Then, (Name of RESIDENTS Designee), shall have the right to take up residence in the Unit at any time up to 25 years from the date of the execution of this Agreement. If they take up residence within this period, they will then have lifetime tenancy privileges as stated in this Agreement.

This Life Tenancy Agreement is exempt from the (State Name) Landlord Tenant Law under the provision of (Location of provision in states statutes). The parties hereto agree solely to be governed by the provisions of this Agreement and the house rules adopted by CENTER. In the event it becomes necessary to employ an attorney to enforce any of the provisions of this Agreement, the prevailing party shall be entitled to receive reasonable attorney's fees and court costs.

ARTICLE II

SERVICES

CENTER agrees to furnish the following as long as Resident carries out his obligations under this Agreement:

A. <u>Lodging</u>: Living accommodations are provided to Unit No. _____ in Building _____ (hereinafter called "Unit"), subject to removal and/or change only as hereinafter provided.

B. <u>Utilities</u>: The utilities (water, electric and heating) will be furnished in connection with the occupancy of the lodging, subject, however, to the availability of such service to CENTER. Telephone service and television cable are the responsibility of individual resident.

C. <u>Furnishings</u>: Within Units, CENTER will provide a stove, refrigerator, dishwasher, washing machine, dryer, and garbage disposal. All other furnishings will be the responsibility of RESIDENTS subject to approval of CENTER.

D. <u>Meals</u>: CENTER may, at the request of RESIDENTS, provide RESIDENTS up to three (3) nutritionally well-balanced meals per day, served only in the dining room. Special diets will be provided only upon request of RESIDENTS and approval of CENTER. All meals requested will be at the expense of the RESIDENTS.

E. <u>Housekeeping</u>: RESIDENTS agree to maintain their Unit in clean, sanitary and orderly condition and to perform all usual housekeeping tasks. Housekeeping services are available upon request of RESIDENTS. All services requested will be at the expense of the RESIDENTS.

F. <u>Laundry</u>: Any and all laundry may be done by RESIDENTS using the washers and dryers provided by CENTER. Items sent out to a laundry and all dry-cleaning will be at RESIDENTS' expense.

G. <u>Other Services</u>: CENTER will also provide the following services and conveniences:

1. Building and ground maintenance and custodial service;

2. Scheduled transportation services;

3. Property taxes, if assessed;

4. Parking for RESIDENTS and guests;

5. Use of common areas and activities areas;

6. Fire detection system; and

7. Laundry facilities.

H. <u>Limitations and Expenses</u>: The CENTER reserves the right of nominal supervision of and, if necessary, may request changes in the furnishings, carpeting, appliances, etc. in the RESIDENTS' Unit when the health, safety and general interest of RESIDENTS are involved.

ARTICLE III

FEES

A. <u>Contribution Fee and Monthly Service Fee</u>: RESIDENTS, by execution of this Agreement, agree to pay CENTER:

1. The sum of (dollar amount written out) ($numeric) as a Contribution Fee, payable in full on or before the date of execution of this Agreement.

2. In addition to the Contribution Fee, the sum of (dollar amount written out) ($numeric) as a Monthly Service Fee, subject to adjustment as hereinafter provided, payable in advance on the first (1st) day of each month with no penalty if paid by the seventh (7th) of the month. If the monthly fee is paid after the seventh (7th) day of the month, a Ten Dollar ($10.00) per day late fee shall be paid by RESIDENTS.

B. <u>Extra Charges</u>: RESIDENTS will be billed by CENTER for any services and supplies obtained for and furnished to RESIDENTS which are not provided for hereunder in return for the regular fees; such bills shall be paid within thirty (30) days after receipt.

C. <u>Changes in Monthly Service Fee</u>: Monthly Service Fees may be adjusted by the center upon thirty (30) days written notice, in order to reflect the actual costs of providing the promised services.

ARTICLE IV

CHANGE IN ACCOMMODATIONS

A. RESIDENTS' Unit may be reassigned under any one of the following conditions:

1. When the RESIDENTS and their Successors are deceased;

2. When the RESIDENTS and their Successors give written notice of termination of residency;

3. When the RESIDENTS and their Successors are, in the sole discretion of the

CENTER, unable to care for his/her own needs.

B. This Agreement may not be terminated except by mutual consent in writing by CENTER and RESIDENTS as outlined in Article IV. A. Until the effective date of termination, RESIDENTS will continue to pay the established Monthly Service Fee together with such amounts as will cover other expenses incurred by or for RESIDENTS and any repairs to or replacement of the property of CENTER caused by RESIDENTS whether willfully or by neglect.

C. RESIDENTS and their Successors who have transferred to a hospital for permanent care may indefinitely retain (his/her/their) Unit provided the Monthly Service Fee is paid until the effective date of termination as outlined in Article IV. A.

ARTICLE V

MISCELLANEOUS ITEMS

A. Representations: All information furnished by RESIDENTS to CENTER in their original application for admission to the CENTER is by this paragraph incorporated as a part of this Agreement and all statements and information thus supplied in this document are and shall be deemed to be true and accurate representations and warranties by RESIDENTS. Any material misstatement therein or any omission of material facts therefrom shall render this Agreement void at the option of the CENTER.

B. Rules and Regulation: RESIDENTS and their Successors hereby agree to abide by CENTER's Rules and Regulations which are incorporated as a part of this Agreement and such reasonable changes of or additions to such Rules and Regulations as may hereafter be adopted by CENTER.

C. CENTER's Liability for RESIDENTS' Debts: CENTER shall not be liable or responsible for any expense, debt or obligation of any kind incurred by RESIDENTS and their Successors.

D. Non-Responsibility for Personal Property: The CENTER shall not be responsible for the loss of any personal property of the RESIDENTS due to any cause. The RESIDENTS agree to indemnify and hold harmless the CENTER for any injury to the person or property of the CENTER or of others resulting from the negligence of the RESIDENTS. The RESIDENTS should have personal liability insurance and should maintain personal property insurance coverage.

E. <u>Property Disposition Upon Transfer or Death</u>:

1. In the event of RESIDENTS' permanent transfer from their Unit to some other facility, all of RESIDENTS' property shall be removed within fifteen (15) days after notification by CENTER to RESIDENTS or their duly named representative.

2. If such property is not removed within the said period of time by RESIDENTS' duly named representative, CENTER shall have the right to remove and store such property for thirty (30) days; thereafter, if such property is not claimed, title to such property shall be vested in CENTER and it shall be disposed of as CENTER, in its sole discretion, deems proper, without any liability to RESIDENTS, their estate or heirs.

F. <u>RESIDENTS' Liability for Damages</u>: RESIDENTS hereby agree to reimburse and hold harmless CENTER for any damages suffered or costs incurred by CENTER as a result of any act of RESIDENTS and/or their guest(s).

G. <u>CENTER's Right to Entry</u>: RESIDENTS agree hereby to give duly authorized employees or agents of CENTER entry into RESIDENTS' Unit at all reasonable times for maintenance and inspection purposes and at any time for emergency purposes.

H. <u>Rights of RESIDENTS—Personal and Subordinate</u>:

1. The right of the RESIDENTS under this Agreement shall not include any proprietary interest in the properties or assets of CENTER. The privileges and services provided RESIDENTS hereunder are personal and may not be sold or assigned nor shall they pass to heirs or personal representatives, except those stated herein.

2. The rights and privileges granted to RESIDENTS by this Agreement do not include right, title or interest in any part of the personal property, land, buildings and improvements owned or administered by the CENTER. RESIDENTS' rights are primarily for services, with a contractual right of occupancy. Any rights, privileges or benefits under this Agreement or any interests or contractual rights of any nature in

the CENTER are and shall be subordinate in priority, right, claim and interest to the lien, charge or security interest of any mortgage, deed of trust or security agreement now or hereafter placed on or affecting any of the CENTER or any interest in the real property or personal property of the CENTER, and to any amendment, modification, replacement, or refunding of any mortgage, deed of trust or security agreement. RESIDENTS agree that upon request, RESIDENTS will execute and deliver any document which is required by the CENTER or by the holder of any such mortgage, deed of trust or security agreement to effect such subordination or to evidence the same.

I. Waivers: The failure of CENTER in any one or more instances to insist upon strict performance, observance or compliance by RESIDENTS with any of the terms or provisions of this Agreement or its waiver of any such breach by RESIDENTS shall not be construed to be a waiver or relinquishment by CENTER of its right to insist upon strict compliance thereafter by RESIDENTS with all terms and conditions of this Agreement. It is understood that CENTER is not bound by any promises or representations made by its representatives or employees which are in any respect at variance with CENTER's Agreement with RESIDENTS as herein set forth.

J. Estate Provisions:

1. Each RESIDENT is required to file in the administrative office of CENTER the name, relationship and address of his next of kin and/or the name and address of the person he wishes to handle his affairs upon his death and to keep such information current.

2. It is understood and agreed that CENTER is not responsible for RESIDENTS' funeral or other burial expenses. RESIDENTS are expected to make such arrangements or to designate some party to make them at their death and to file evidence of such arrangement in CENTER's administrative office.

K. Inability to Handle Personal Affairs: In the event RESIDENTS become unable to handle their personal or financial affairs and have made no other valid arrangement with regard to such circumstance (which is encouraged), RESIDENTS hereby request any court of competent jurisdiction to appoint _____ as conservator and guardian of their person and/or property; or, in the event such named person is unwilling or unable to serve, then to name an alternate to such position in keeping with the requirements of law.

L. Guests: RESIDENTS may welcome such visitors as they wish for visits in their Unit upon such reasonable terms and conditions as CENTER may establish.

1. RESIDENTS may have guests on the premises, but no guests may stay more than fifteen (15) days without the prior written approval of CENTER.

2. RESIDENTS shall be responsible for all meals and other costs incurred in connection with such guests.

3. No visitor who has any contagious illness or disease is permitted to visit in CENTER.

4. RESIDENTS are responsible for any injury to others or damage to the property of others or of CENTER by their guest(s).

M. Unit Alterations: RESIDENTS may, at their expense and with the approval of CENTER, effect modifications of a minor nature to the Unit. Modifications which result in permanent installations such as shelving, drapery rods, etc., immediately become the property of CENTER and shall remain in the Unit upon being vacated by RESIDENTS.

N. Binding Effects: This agreement and all rights and obligations hereunder shall be binding upon CENTER and RESIDENTS and their Successors.

O. Attorney's Fees: In the event suit is brought (or arbitration instituted) or an attorney is retained by any party to this Agreement to enforce the terms of this Agreement or to collect any money due hereunder, or to collect money damages for breach hereof, the prevailing party shall be entitled to recover, in addition to any other remedy, reimbursement for reasonable attorney's fees, court costs, costs of investigation and other related expenses incurred in connection therewith.

P. Notices: Any notice to any party under this Agreement shall be in writing and shall be effective on the earlier of (i) the date when received by such party, or (ii) the date which is three (3) days after mailing (postage prepaid) by certified or registered mail, return receipt requested, to the party.

Q.   Time: Time is of the essence of this Agreement and each and every provision hereof. Any extension of time granted for the performance of any duty under this Agreement shall not be considered an extension of time for the performance of any other duty under this Agreement.

R.   Governing Law: This Agreement shall be deemed to be made under, and shall be construed in accordance with and shall be governed by, the laws of the State of (State Name), and (subject to any provision of this Agreement) providing for mandatory arbitration suit to enforce any provision of this Agreement or to obtain any remedy with respect hereto may be brought in Superior Court, (County), (State), and for this purpose each party hereby expressly and irrevocably consents to the jurisdiction of said court.

S.   Construction: The language in all parts of this Agreement shall in all cases be construed as a whole according to its fair meaning and not strictly for nor against any party. The neuter gender includes the masculine and feminine. It is mutually agreed that in the event any term, covenant or condition herein contained is held to be invalid or void by any court of competent jurisdiction, the invalidity of any such term, covenant or condition shall in no way affect any other term, covenant or condition herein contained.

T.   Severability: If any provision of this Agreement is declared void or unenforceable, such provision shall be deemed severed from this Agreement; and the remaining portions of the Agreement shall remain in full force and effect.

U.   Additional Acts and Documents: Each party hereto agrees to do all such things and take all such actions, and to make, execute and deliver such other documents and instruments, as shall be reasonably requested to carry out the provisions, intent and purpose of this Agreement.

V.   Integration Clause; Oral Modification: This Agreement represents the entire agreement of the parties with respect to the subject matter hereof, and all agreements entered into prior hereto are revoked and superseded by this Agreement, and no representations, warranties, inducements or oral agreements have been made by any of the parties except as expressly set forth herein, or in other contemporaneous written agreements. This Agreement may not be changed, modified or rescinded except in writing, signed by all parties hereto, and any attempt at oral modifications of this Agreement shall be void and of no effect.

X. Indemnity: Each party to this Agreement agrees to indemnify each other party, and hold it harmless, from and against all claims, damages, costs and expenses (including attorney's fees) attributable, directly or indirectly, to the breach by such indemnifying party herein or in any instrument delivered pursuant hereto or in connection with the transactions contemplated hereby.

IN WITNESS WHEREOF, the parties hereto have executed this Residence Agreement the day and year first above written.

(*Name*) _____

an (*State*) _____ corporation.

BY_____

TITLE_____

_____
RESIDENT

_____
RESIDENT

_____
SUCCESSOR

_____
SUCCESSOR

EXHIBIT 5

LIFE CARE AGREEMENT FOR INDEPENDENT LIVING

This Agreement is made and entered into this_____ day of _____, 199____,

by and between _____

hereinafter collectively referred to as the Resident, and (Name of Corporation), a

profit/nonprofit corporation, hereinafter referred to as the "Corporation."

Section I: Entrance Fees and Rights

A. The Resident having made application to establish residency in the (Name of Facility) (the "Community") and upon acceptance of the application by the Corporation, agrees to comply with the policies of the Corporation and further, understands that such residency shall be subject to the following terms and conditions.

B. The Confidential Data Application submitted by the Resident to the Corporation is incorporated herein and by this reference is made a part of this Agreement.

C. The (Facility Name) Care Program, as currently in effect, is incorporated herein and made a part of this Agreement.

D. As a condition of residency, the Resident must be in good enough health at the time of establishing residency to maintain himself/herself in the living unit without assistance, unless this condition has been waived in writing by the Corporation.

E. The Resident agrees to pay the Corporation an Entrance Fee of $_____, for the right of residency, in living unit type:_____

   No._____, and an additional Entrance Fee of $_____ for each additional party to this Agreement.

F. The total Entrance Fees (hereinafter called Entrance Fee) is $_____ and is payable as follows: a deposit of $_____ payable with the execution of this Agreement and the balance of $_____ payable at the earlier of (a) the date the living unit is first available for occupancy, notice of which shall be given by the Corporation to the Resident at least sixty (60) days in advance of such date, or (b) the date on which the Resident moves into the living unit or otherwise establishes residency in the Community.

G. The Resident shall have a period of seven (7) days beginning with the first full calendar day following the last to occur of: (1) the execution of the Residence Agreement, (2) the payment of Entrance Fee deposit, or (3) receipt of a copy of Corporation's most recent annual report, on file with the (Name of State) Department of Insurance, within which to rescind this Agreement without penalty or further obligation. In the event of such rescision, all money or property paid or transferred by Resident to Corporation shall be fully refunded by Corporation to Resident. No Resident shall be required to move into the facility until after the expiration of the seven (7) day rescision period.

H. In the event the Resident (or if there is more than one, then both of them) should be deceased or in the event the Resident (or if there is more than one, then one of them) should become incapacitated prior to establishing residency in the Community so that he/she no longer would qualify for residency under the terms of this Agreement, this Agreement shall be terminated and the Corporation shall refund to the Resident or his/her legal representative, all funds deposited. However, should the Resident give written notice of cancellation of this Agreement for any other reason, after the expiration of the seven (7) day rescision period and prior to establishing residency in the Community, the Corporation shall refund to the Resident all funds deposited less an application fee of $500.00 included in the deposit.

In all cases, the Corporation shall not be required to refund any part of costs specifically incurred by the Corporation, at the request of the Resident and which have been set forth in an agreement signed by both parties.

I. In consideration for the Entrance Fee paid by the Resident, the Corporation agrees that said Resident shall have the right of residency in the Community in the assigned living unit, including admittance to the Health Care Center, subject to the conditions and/or cancellation provisions hereinafter provided. All furnishings and decorations other than major appliances and standard painting and carpeting provided by the Corporation, shall be the responsibility of the Resident.

J. If this Agreement is executed by two parties, it is agreed that upon termination of residence in the Community by one Resident for any cause, all rights and obligations herein shall vest in the remaining Resident.

K. Occupancy of the reserved living unit may occur after the seven (7) day rescision period and after the payment of the Entrance Fee, unless otherwise stipulated in writing.

L. If the Resident passes away after taking residency in the Community, the obligation of the Corporation pursuant to this Agreement, including the Entrance Fee, shall be fulfilled, and there shall be no repayment of any portion of the Entrance Fee.

M. The rights and privileges of Resident under this Agreement to the living accommodations, facilities and services are personal to Resident and cannot be transferred or assigned by act of the Resident, or by any proceeding at law or otherwise. No person other than Resident may occupy or use the accommodations covered by this Agreement, except with the written approval of the Corporation.

N. THE RIGHTS AND PRIVILEGES GRANTED TO RESIDENT BY THIS AGREEMENT DO NOT INCLUDE RIGHT, TITLE OR INTEREST IN ANY PART OF THE PERSONAL PROPERTY, LAND, BUILDINGS AND IMPROVEMENTS OWNED OR ADMINISTERED BY THE CORPORATION. RESIDENTS' RIGHTS ARE PRIMARILY FOR SERVICES, WITH A CONTRACTUAL RIGHT OF OCCUPANCY. ANY RIGHTS, PRIVILEGES OR BENEFITS UNDER THIS AGREEMENT OR ANY INTERESTS OR CONTRACTUAL RIGHTS OF ANY NATURE IN THE COMMUNITY ARE AND SHALL BE SUBORDINATE IN PRIORITY, RIGHT, CLAIM AND INTEREST TO THE LIEN, CHARGE OR SECURITY INTEREST OF ANY MORTGAGE, DEED OF TRUST OR SECURITY AGREEMENT NOW OR HEREAFTER PLACED ON OR AFFECTING ANY OF THE CORPORATION OR THE COMMUNITY OR ANY INTEREST IN THE REAL PROPERTY OR PERSONAL PROPERTY OF THE CORPORATION, AND TO ANY AMENDMENT,

MODIFICATION, REPLACEMENT, OR REFUNDING OF ANY MORTGAGE, DEED OF TRUST OR SECURITY AGREEMENT. A RESIDENT AGREES THAT UPON REQUEST, THE RESIDENT WILL EXECUTE AND DELIVER ANY DOCUMENT WHICH IS REQUIRED BY THE CORPORATION OR BY THE HOLDER OF ANY SUCH MORTGAGE, DEED OF TRUST, OR SECURITY AGREEMENT TO EFFECT SUCH SUBORDINATION OR TO EVIDENCE THE SAME.

Section II: Services and Fees

A. A Monthly Service Fee for the assigned living unit is due and payable in advance on the first day of each month. The Board of Trustees of the Corporation will annually review, and upon thirty days written notice, may adjust the Monthly Service Fee as deemed necessary.

B. For the payment of the Monthly Service Fee, the Corporation offers its Residents the following services and conveniences: (1) one meal per day; (2) tray service when approved by Administration for medical reasons; (3) building and grounds maintenance and custodial service; (4) weekly flat laundry service; (5) scheduled transportation service; (6) all utilities including air conditioning, except telephone and cable television; (7) real estate taxes, if assessed; (8) basic or skilled nursing care as outlined in Section III; (9) adult day health care, residential aide and social services; (10) special diets when ordered by a physician; (11) planned activities—social, cultural, recreational, and spiritual—for those who wish to participate; (12) standard cleaning of the living unit every other week; (13) parking for Residents and guests; (14) use of common areas and activities areas and private dining room; (15) emergency call system; (16) master television antenna; (17) community security; (18) fire detection system; (19) services of a chaplain; and (20) laundromats for personal laundry.

C. Additional services and conveniences are available to Residents on an extra charge basis, including but not limited to the following: (1) beautician and barber services; (2) physical therapy; (3) guest meals; (4) additional meals for Residents; and (5) other optional services reasonably available, which may be requested by the Resident.

Section III: Nursing Care

A. In consideration for payment of the Monthly Service Fee, and upon admittance to the Health Care Center, the Resident shall receive intermediate or skilled nursing care in a semi-private room, providing the Resident, if eligible, is currently covered by Medicare, Parts A and B (Basic and Supplemental) and at least one supplementary health insurance policy. If proceeds from Medicare and/or supplementary health insurance policies are allowable for nursing care provided in the Health Care Center, these shall be paid to the Corporation.

B. This nursing care is provided without limitation as to the length of time the Resident may be provided such care, except that the following conditions are specifically excluded: psychiatric care, dangerously contagious diseases, legal insanity, and any other condition requiring services prohibited under the license of the Health Care Center.

C. The Resident shall engage the services of his/her own physician, at Resident's expense, for consultation and treatment if needed. The Corporation will attempt to contact the Resident's physician in an emergency but should this not be possible, the Corporation may consult its own consulting physician or effect emergency admittance of the Resident in a local hospital.

D. The Resident is personally responsible for the cost of sundries, medicine, ancillary items, medical and nonmedical extras, drugs, personal articles, meals not provided by Monthly Service Fee, and the cost of any health insurance policies.

E. In the event the Resident is affected with a dangerously contagious disease, or becomes mentally or emotionally disturbed to the degree that his or her presence in the Community shall be deemed detrimental to the health, safety or peaceful lodging of other residents, the Corporation shall have the authority to transfer the Resident to an appropriate hospital. This determination shall be made by the Corporation Administrator in consultation with the Resident's personal physician and a member of the Resident's family or guardian. If the Resident is transferred from the Community pursuant to this paragraph, reimbursement to the Resident will be made as described in Section IV.

F.   In the event it should be necessary for a Resident to become a permanent patient in the Health Care Center (such change of status is normally made only after stay in the Health Care Center has exceeded three months and/or the Administrator has determined, in consultation with the Resident's physician and family or guardian that it shall not be feasible for the Resident to resume unassisted living in the living unit), the Corporation shall have the right to reassign the living unit; however, a similar or alternate unit shall be made available in the Community should the Resident recover sufficiently to resume unassisted living.

Section IV: Termination and Refund

A.   The Resident shall have the right to terminate this Agreement after establishing residency in the Community, upon fulfilling the following terms and conditions: (1) The Resident is in good enough health to live without assistance in his/her living unit; (2) the Resident gives ninety (90) days written notice; and (3) the Monthly Service Fee is paid in full to the end of the ninety (90) days notice. Refunds shall be made as described in Paragraph IV. C.

B.   The Corporation may terminate the Resident's residency upon a thirty (30) days written notice to the Resident and upon a showing of good cause that the Resident is not complying with the policies of the Corporation and/or is creating a disturbance within the community detrimental to the health, safety, or peaceful lodging of others. In the event a Resident's residency is thus terminated, refund shall be made as described in Paragraph C of this section.

C.   In the event that residency is terminated other than by death, pursuant to the terms of this Agreement, the Corporation shall refund to the Resident the Entrance Fee paid subject to all the following terms: (1) The Corporation shall retain 10% of the Entrance

Fee paid plus 1% for each month or portion that residency has been established; (2) the Corporation shall retain any unreimbursed expenses incurred for the Resident's care in the Health Care Center or outside nursing home during his/her residency and any other costs which may have been incurred at the request of the Resident. The Resident's care expense in the Health Care Center will be calculated on the basis of the semi-private daily charge for a non-resident patient current at date of termination.

D. The Resident agrees to make payments herein provided for at the time and in the manner specified by the Corporation; and upon failure to do so, the Corporation shall have the right to terminate this Agreement if any such payment shall be in default for more than ninety (90) days.

E. It is the declared policy of the Corporation that a Resident's residency shall not be terminated solely by reason of financial inability of the Resident to pay the Monthly Service Fee, provided the Resident has applied for and established the facts which justify special financial consideration, and such subsidy can be granted or continued without impairing the ability of the Corporation to obtain its objectives while operating on a sound financial basis. In the event such subsidy is granted by the Corporation, any deficiency amount owing to the Corporation by reason thereof shall be due and payable at such time as the Resident shall have sufficient funds therefor and otherwise shall be due and payable from and enforceable against the Resident's estate. Such consideration shall be granted at the sole discretion of the Board of Trustees of the Corporation.

F. Within thirty (30) days after establishing residency in the Community, the Resident should update his/her will to include the disposition of all furniture, possessions and property used or kept by the Resident, upon the death or permanent transfer of the Resident to the Health Care Center. If said personal property is not claimed within thirty (30) days after the unit is vacated, then the Corporation shall have the immediate right to dispose of said personal property unless other arrangements are made with the Administrator. The Resident or his representative shall be entitled to any proceeds remaining after the payment of all expenses.

Section V: Miscellaneous

A. The Corporation shall not be responsible for the loss of any personal property of the Resident due to any cause. The Resident agrees to indemnify and hold harmless the Corporation for any injury to the person or property of the Corporation or of others resulting from the negligence of the Resident. Each Resident should have personal liability insurance and should maintain personal property insurance coverage.

B. The Resident attests that the information contained in the Confidential Data Application is true and complete disclosure of all material facts which would affect approval for residency in the Community. The Resident further agrees that should there be any material change in Resident's financial, physical, or mental condition prior to establishing residency, it is the responsibility of the Resident to so inform the Administration. Failure to do so will constitute grounds for the Corporation to terminate this Agreement and the Resident's residency.

C. This Agreement, together with the Confidential Data Application and the Life Care Program, contains the entire agreement between the parties hereto and no amendment or addendum is valid unless contained in a writing executed by the Corporation and the Resident.

D. The invalidity or amendment of any restriction, condition, or other provision of this Agreement, or of any part of the same, shall not impair or affect in any way the validity, enforceability, or effect of the rest of this Agreement.

IN WITNESS WHEREOF, the parties have hereto affixed their signatures this _____ day
of _____, 199____.

_____
Resident

_____   _____
Witness and Agent   Resident

Approved this _____ day of   _____

_____, 199_____.   _____
                                                          (Facility Name)

                                                          _____
                                                          (Corporation Name)
                                                          Its Duly Authorized Representative

EXHIBIT 6

RESIDENTIAL CARE APPLICATION

Name_____ Date _____

Address_____ City/State/Zip _____

Phone_____ How long have you lived at your present address?_____

Birthdate_____ Birthplace_____ Social Security # _____

Married_____ Single_____ Widow/Widower _____

Pre-retirement occupation _____

Church presently attending_____ City/State _____

Pastor's name_____ Phone _____

Do you think you can adjust to group living?   Yes_____   No_____

Will you have a pet at (name of facility)?   Yes_____   No_____

Do you plan to bring your car?   Yes_____   No_____

Do you plan to take meals in the dining room?   Yes_____   No_____

HEALTH HISTORY

At (name of facility), we reserve the right to require a medical examination.

Physician's name_____ Phone_____

Address _____

Do you consider your general health to be: Good_____   Fair_____   Poor_____

Any special health problems? Explain: _____

_____

Do you smoke?   Yes_____   No_____

Present Medications:_____

_____

List medication allergies: _____

_____

Do you use an assistive device to get around? Cane_____ Walker_____ Wheelchair_____

Other _____

Hospital you prefer _____

FINANCIAL INFORMATION

Information listed below is confidential and will not be given to any individual, government agency, or any other group without the permission of the applicant.

Are you enrolled in the Medicare Program?   No_____   Yes_____:

Medicare #_____   Plan A_____ Plan B_____

Do you have additional hospital or and/or Medicare insurance? If so, give name and describe coverage:

_____

Any insurance coverage with an ambulance service?   No_____   Yes_____:

Name_____ Phone _____

Name of Funeral Home_____ Phone _____

Does someone other than you administer your finances?   No_____   Yes_____:

Name_____ Phone _____

Address _____ City/State/Zip _____

Do you have a legally appointed person, such as a Power of Attorney, to make decisions if you become unable to do so?   No_____   Yes_____:

Name_____ Phone _____

Address_____ City/State/Zip _____

Please list your approximate monthly income:

Social Security: $_____

Pension: $_____

Other: $_____

Please list your assets so that (name of facility) may be assured of your ability to finance your stay:

Cash, (Savings & Checking): $_____   Other Real Estate: $_____

Stock, Bonds, etc.: $_____   Automobile: $_____

Notes Receivable: $_____   Life Insurance: $_____

Home: $_____   Other:_____ $_____

Can your family contribute to your support, if necessary?   Yes_____   No_____

How do you plan to pay the current monthly rate? (Check one or more)

Personally_____ Family Members_____ Social Security _____

I agree to pay for all medicines _____ and doctor's fees _____.

PERSONAL REFERENCES

Please give names and addresses of two reliable persons not related to you:

Name_____ Phone _____

Address_____ City/State/Zip _____

Name_____ Phone _____

Address_____ City/State/Zip _____

List the names and addresses of relatives we could contact in the event of an emergency, in the order you want them called:

Name_____ Phone _____

Address_____ City/State/Zip _____

Relationship_____

Name_____ Phone _____

Address_____ City/State/Zip _____

Relationship_____

Name_____ Phone _____

Address_____ City/State/Zip _____

Relationship_____

What one major factor most influenced your decisions to reside at (name of facility)?

_____

I do hereby make application for residency at (name of facility). I am in full sympathy with the ideals, goals, rules and regulations and agree to wholeheartedly cooperate with the management according to the statements as set forth in the Lease Agreement and House Rules. I agree that the rates may be evaluated and changed in accordance with changes in the future economy.

This application is made with the understanding that the financial and health statements contained herein may be investigated by action of (name of facility). I agree to make other living arrangements if the management decides that my behavior is detrimental to the peace and harmony of (name of facility) or if my health needs require a higher level of care as determined by (name of facility).

_____   _____

Applicant   Date

EXHIBIT 7

RECORD OF ADMISSION FOR NURSING HOME CARE

(Name of Facility) _____

(Address of Facility) _____

Identification Summary

Patient Name (Last) (First) (Middle/Maiden)	Admission Number	Sex	Race	Religion

Usual Residence—Street (if Rural, give location)	Home Phone	Date of Birth	Age

City-Town (Precinct No. If applicable)	State	County	Zip Code	Marital Status M S W D Sep. Is Spouse living? Yes No

Date Admitted	Time Admitted A.M. P.M.	Room No.	Previous Adm. Date if applicable	Previous Admission No.	Birthplace

Attending Physician	Address	Phone(s)	Citizen of what Country

Alternate Physician	Address	Phone(s)	Social Security Number

Dentist	Address	Phone	Medicare Number

Next of Kin or Responsible Person	Address	Phone	Relation-ship	Welfare Claim Number (if applicable)

Person to Notify in Emergency	Address	Phone	Relation-ship	Served in U.S. Armed Forces? Yes No Unknown

Mortuary to Notify	Address	Phone	War or Dates of Service

Church/Synagogue	Address	Phone	Usual Occupation (most of working life)

Name of Insurance Company	Address	Certificate/Policy Number	Business—Industry

Admitted From (If institution, give Name, Address and Phone)	Name of Patient's Spouse (If wife give maiden name)

How Transferred	Referred By	If admitted from institution, give Dates of Stay	Patient's Father's Name

ALLERGIES — Patient's Mother's Maiden Name

Admission Summary

Primary Admitting Diagnosis:

Secondary Admitting Diagnosis:

Rehabilitation Potential:

Prognosis:

This patient has been informed of his physical and mental condition and plan of treatment.
☐ Yes   ☐ No
If no, explain _____

*Physician's Signature _____

*If this section is not signed by the physician, this summary information has been transcribed from document(s) contained in this patient's clinical record which appropriately bear the physician's (date) signature. Signature of Transcribing Nurse_____ Date_____

Discharge Summary

Date of Discharge	Time	Accompanied by (Name, Address, Relationship)

Place Discharged To	Address	City	State	Phone

Condition on Discharge: Recovered   Improved   Unimproved   Declined Treatment   Other (Explain)

Discharge Diagnosis:

Course of Treatment:

Prognosis:

*Physician's Signature _____

*If this section is not signed by the physician, this summary information has been transcribed from document(s) contained in this patient's clinical record which appropriately bear the physician's (date) signature. Signature of Transcribing Nurse_____ Date_____

Patient's Name	Case Number	**Admission/Discharge Summary**

Record of Admission Authorizations

1. **Permission to Summon a Physician or Dentist in Case of Emergency:**
   In order to assure proper patient care, permission is granted the professional staff of the admitting facility to summon a physician or dentist of their choice in the event that the patient's own physician or dentist or designated alternate is not readily available. It is agreed that payment of fees for services of said physician and/or dentist is the responsibility of the patient.

2. **Waiver of Liability – Smoking:**
   It is hereby acknowledged that the patient has been advised not to smoke while in the facility or on the grounds without direct supervision of an attendant employed by the facility. We do hereby agree that if the patient is injured or any property of the patient is damaged or destroyed by reason of smoking by the patient, the admitting facility shall not be liable for and is hereby held harmless from all liability for such injury, damage or destruction.

3. **Waiver of Liability – Bedrails:**
   It is hereby acknowledged that the patient has been advised that while at the admitting facility, bedrails should be used for the patient's own protection and safety. We do hereby agree that if the patient is injured in any way while declining use of bedrails, the admitting facility is hereby absolved and released from any and all liability for any injury or damage.

4. **Waiver of Liability – Electrical Appliances and Personal Furnishings:**
   It is hereby agreed that in using personally obtained furnishings or electrical appliances in the patient's room while in the admitting facility, the use thereof is at the patient's risk and the facility is hereby absolved and released of any and all responsibility and liability for burns, injuries, property damage or losses which may result from or because of said appliances/furnishings.

5. **Release of Responsibility for Leaving Premises Without Approval:**
   It is hereby certified that the patient is being admitted to the admitting facility on his or her own volition and the facility, its personnel and the attending physician is absolved and released of any responsibility if the patient should leave the premises of the facility for any reason whatsoever without consent of the attending physician and notice to the facility management.

6. **Authorization for Release of Information:**
   The admitting institution is hereby authorized to furnish and release, in accordance with facility policy, such professional and clinical information as may be necessary for the completion of my hospitalization claims by valid third party agents or agencies from the medical records compiled during my confinement. The admitting facility is hereby released from all legal liability that may arise from the release of said information.

7. **Authorization for Release of Body:**
   In the event the patient expires, the admitting facility is hereby authorized to release the body to the mortuary specified on the reverse.

8. **Treatment Consent:**
   Patient at all times shall be under the care of his attending physician and the facility is not liable for any act of omission in following the instructions of said physician who is neither the employer nor agent of the facility. Patient consents to examinations, treatments, medications, and procedures prescribed for the patient by his physician, his designated alternate, or by any other physician in case of emergency.

9. **General Duty Nursing:**
   The institution provides general duty nursing care. If the patient is in such condition as to need continuous or special duty nursing care, it is agreed that such must be arranged by the patient or his/her legal representative or physician and that the institution shall in no way be responsible for failure to provide the same and is hereby released from any and all liability arising from the fact that said patient is not provided with such additional care.

The above nine (9) articles are hereby understood and meet with my (our) approval. I (we) acknowledge receipt of a copy of this document.

Signed:

_____   _____ / _____
Witness   Patient   Date

_____   _____ / _____ / _____
Witness   Other Person Responsible   Date   Relationship

Exhibit 8

NURSING CENTER
ADMISSION AGREEMENT

THE _____(NAME OF FACILITY)_____ (hereinafter referred to as "Nursing Center") and _____ (hereinafter referred to as "Responsible Party"), hereby agree to the following terms for the care of _____.

ADMISSION DATE _____.

Should the Resident be admitted under Medicare Part A, the Responsible Party agrees to pay the co-insurance portion of the Medicare bill as mandated by Federal Rules and Regulations.

Should the Resident not be Medicare, County, or V.A. eligible, the Responsible Party agrees to pay daily, in full consideration for care and services rendered, the following rates:

A.   **TOTAL ROOM AND BOARD** $ _____

          Other $ _____

          TOTAL $ _____

Ancillary charges including incontinency aids, special feeding and nursing supplies, equipment rental, maintenance therapy, and other items as may be requested by the physician, Responsible Party, or Resident will be assessed monthly and charged accordingly without prior notice.

B. **RESPONSIBLE PARTY CHARGES:** The following items are the financial responsibility of the Responsible Party: Pharmacy, Oxygen, Beauty Shop, Nursing Supplies necessary for the care of the Resident, and Physician charges.

C. **RATE INCREASES:** It is understood and agreed between the Nursing Center and the Responsible Party that the total daily rate charges for a particular level of care is subject to change from time to time. It is further agreed between the Nursing Center and the Responsible Party that if and when the above specified charge is increased, the Responsible Party will be given thirty (30) days written notice of change.

Upon receipt of said notice, the Responsible Party may, if he or she does not wish to incorporate the new price terms into this agreement, remove the Resident from the Nursing Center and terminate this agreement pursuant to the notice provisions of Paragraph E. Otherwise, the Responsible Party may continue to take advantage of the services rendered by the Nursing Center, in which case the Responsible Party agrees that the new charge will automatically become part of this agreement, superseding the figure indicated above, upon expiration of the above referenced thirty (30) days notice period.

D. INITIAL BILLING: The Nursing Center requires an advance payment equal to thirty (30) days Total Room and Board at the time of admission. Thereafter, billing will be based on the calendar month with payment required in advance.

E. TRANSFER NOTICE: When a Resident is to be transferred on a non-emergency basis from the Nursing Center, the Nursing Center shall be given (10) days written notice of such transfer, otherwise the Responsible Party shall be charged for those ten (10) days.

F. DISCHARGE TIME: Routine discharge time is 10:00 A.M., and there will be no charge for that day. If a late discharge is desired, the arrangements must be made twenty-four (24) hours in advance.

G. DAY OF ADMISSION: In order to safeguard the well-being of other Residents and Staff, any Resident who becomes too difficult for Staff to handle appropriately or who fails to pay the rate agreed upon at the specified intervals, will be required to transfer to another facility immediately. The Nursing Center will work with the Responsible Party to expedite such transfers.

H. REFUNDS: When a Resident is discharged, any resulting credit from the advance billing will be determined less any unpaid charges. The refund will be mailed to the Resident or Responsible Party within two to four weeks.

I. ROOM TRANSFER: Should the Resident be admitted under Medicare Part A, the Responsible Party agrees to the required room transfer when needed to comply with Federal Rules and Regulations. Should the Resident be non-Medicare, permission is also given to move the Resident within the facility to better accommodate compatibility and/or medical need. Prior notification to the Resident or Responsible Party will be given.

J. ITEMS OF VALUE: It is recommended that the Responsible Party keep all valuable items for the Resident. The Nursing Center cannot be responsible for any items left in the

Resident's room, including money, dentures, eyeglasses, approved appliances or sentimental items.

K. PERSONAL CLOTHING: All personal clothing must be marked prior to being brought into the Nursing Center. The Nursing center assumes no responsibility for lost or missing clothing during the stay of the Resident.

L. ALTCS ROLL-OVER: If a Resident admitted to the Nursing Center becomes eligible for ALTCS within the first year, the Nursing Center cannot guarantee bed availability for the Resident.

M. SUMMARY: In the event the Responsible Party fails to abide by or fulfill his or her duties under any provision of this Agreement, the Responsible Party agrees that in addition to any other remedy which the Nursing Center may have at law or equity, all amounts incurred up to that time for services rendered by the Nursing Center will become immediately due and payable and said amount shall bear interest at the rate of 18% per annum until paid. In addition, the Responsible Party agrees to pay all costs and fees incurred in the enforcement of any of the Responsible Party's obligations under this Agreement.

_____   _____
Resident/Responsible Party   **(Name of Facility) Admissions Director**

_____   _____
Address   **Date**

_____
City   **State**   **Zip**

Exhibit 9

LIVING WILL DECLARATION

DECLARATION MADE THIS _____ DAY OF _____ (month, year), I, _____, being of sound mind, willfully and voluntarily make known my desire that my dying not be artificially prolonged under the circumstances set forth below and declare that:

If at any time I should have an incurable injury, disease, or illness certified to be a terminal condition by two physicians who have personally examined me, one of whom is my attending physician, and the physicians have determined that my death will occur unless life-sustaining procedures are used, and if the application of life-sustaining procedures would serve only to artificially prolong the dying process, I direct that life-sustaining procedures be withheld or withdrawn and that I be permitted to die naturally with only the performance of medical procedures deemed necessary to provide me with comfort care.

I further direct that if at any time I should be in a permanent vegetative state or an irreversible coma as certified by two physicians who have personally examined me, one of whom is my attending physician, and the physicians determine that the application of life-sustaining procedures, including artificially administered food and fluids, will only artificially prolong my life in a permanent vegetative state or irreversible coma, I direct that these procedures, including the administration of food and fluids, be withheld or withdrawn and that I be permitted to die naturally with only the administration of medication to alleviate pain or the performance of other medical procedures necessary to provide me with comfort care.

In the absence of my ability to give directions regarding the use of life-sustaining procedures, it is my intention that this declaration be honored by my family and attending physician as the final expression of my legal right to refuse medical or surgical treatment and accept the consequences from such refusal.

I understand the full impact of this declaration and I have emotional and mental capacity to make this declaration.

Signed _____

City, County and State of Residence _____

The declarant is personally known to me, and I believe him/her to be of sound mind.

Witness_____   Witness _____

Date _____   Date _____

Exhibit 10

DURABLE POWER OF ATTORNEY FOR HEALTH CARE

WARNING TO PERSON EXECUTING THIS DOCUMENT

This is an important legal document. It creates a durable power of attorney for health care. Before executing this document, you should know these important facts:

1. This document gives the person you designate as your attorney in fact the power to make health care decisions for you, subject to any limitations or statement of your desires that you include in this document. The power to make health care decisions for you may include consent, refusal of consent, or withdrawal of consent to any care, treatment, service, or procedure to maintain, diagnose, or treat a physical or mental condition. You may state in this document any types of treatment or placements that you do not desire.

2. The person you designate in this document has a duty to act consistently with your desires as stated in this document or otherwise made known or, if your desires are unknown, to act in your best interests.

3. Except as you otherwise specify in this document, the power of the person you designate to make health care decisions for you may include the power to give consent to your doctor to withhold treatment or to stop treatment which would keep you alive.

4. Unless you specify a shorter period in this document, this power will exist for seven years from the date you execute this document and, if you are unable to make health care decisions for yourself at the time when this seven-year period ends, this power will continue to exist until the time when you become able to make health care decisions for yourself.

5. Notwithstanding this document, you have the right to make medical and other health care decisions for yourself so long as you can give informed consent with respect to the particular decision. In addition, no treatment may be given to you over your objection, and health care necessary to keep you alive may not be stopped if you object.

6. You have the right to revoke the appointment of the person designated in this document by notifying that person of the revocation orally or in writing.

7. You have the right to revoke the authority granted to the person designated in this document to make health care decisions for you by notifying the treating physician, hospital, or other health care provider orally or in writing.

8. The person designated in this document to make health care decisions for you has the right to examine your medical records and to consent to their disclosure unless you limit this right in this document.

9. If there is anything in this document that you do not understand, you should ask a lawyer to explain it to you.

This power of attorney will not be valid for making health care decisions unless it is either (1) signed by two qualified witnesses who are personally known to you and who are present when you sign or acknowledge your signature or (2) acknowledged before a notary public in _____.

Read:

Date: _____   _____

                                                         Signature

Certificate of Acknowledgement of Notary Public

State of _____   )

) ss.

County of _____   )

On _____, _____, before me, the undersigned, a Notary Public in and for the State of _____, personally appeared _____, proved to me on the basis of satisfactory evidence to be the person whose name is subscribed to the foregoing Durable Power of Attorney for Health Care; and _____ acknowledged that _____ executed the same as Principal thereof.

I declare under penalty of perjury that the person whose name is subscribed to this Durable Power of Attorney for Health Care appears to be of sound mind and under no duress, fraud, or undue influence.

WITNESS my hand and official seal.

_____

                              Notary Public

DURABLE POWER OF ATTORNEY FOR HEALTH CARE

This is a DURABLE POWER OF ATTORNEY FOR HEALTH CARE under _____ Code of the State of _____, beginning with section _____ of said Code.

1. *Designation of Attorney-in-Fact and Alternate.*

I, _____ (now residing at _____, _____, _____) appoint _____ (now residing at _____, _____, _____), to serve as my Attorney-in-Fact to make health care decisions for me as authorized in this document and in _____ Civil Code sections _____ et seq. If, for any reason, _____ is unable to serve as my Attorney-in-Fact, I appoint _____ (now residing at _____, _____, _____) to serve as such Attorney-in-Fact.

2. *Statement of Authority Granted.*

In the event that I am incapable of giving informed consent to health care decisions, I grant to my Attorney-in-Fact the authority to make all health care decisions for me, as authorized by and pursuant to _____ Code sections _____ et seq. This grant of authority is subject to any special instructions that appear in Paragraph 3 below.

3. *Special Instructions.*

   a. *Life Prolonging Treatment.* In exercising authority under this document, my Attorney-in-Fact should bear in mind my attitude toward the use of life prolonging treatment, which is reflected in my choice of one of the two following statements:

   (1) I do not believe that the use of every known treatment and procedure designed to sustain life is warranted in every situation. It is my belief that the decision to use life prolonging treatment depends upon the likelihood of a return to normal functioning, the suffering that the treatment will cause, and the quality of life that will result if the treatment is given. I think that these factors must be weighed in each individual case and I have appointed my attorney in fact in this document to perform this function. [_____]

   (2) I believe that no person has the right to decide to withhold medical treatment from another person, when treatment is available that may extend life. I think that one person cannot judge the quality of another person's life. By signing this document, I intend to delegate to my attorney in fact the power to make health care decisions should I become incompetent, but that power does not extend to decisions regarding life prolonging treatment. [_____]

   b. *Additional Instructions.* In exercising authority under this document, my Attorney-in-Fact is subject to the following additional instructions:

   _____

   _____

   _____

   _____

   _____

   _____

4. *Duration.*

   This durable power of attorney for health care will last seven years from the date that I sign it. If I am unable to make health care decisions for myself when this power of attorney would otherwise expire, the authority I have granted herein shall continue in full force until such time (if ever) as I regain the ability to make my own health care decisions.

5. *Signature.*

   I hereby sign my name to this form, which creates a durable power of attorney for health care.

_____   _____
         (Signature)   (Date)

From Paul A. Gordon, J. D., *Project Documents and Forms*, vol. 2 in *Developing Retirement Communities* (New York: John Wiley & Sons, Inc.).

EXHIBIT 11

Table of Comparison for Long-Term Care Insurance Policies

Standard Features of Nursing Home Policies

Company	AMEX	Bankers United	CNA	PFL Life	Transport
Best rating	A+	A	A++	A	A
Assets	$945 MIL	$637 MIL	$36 BILLION	$4.4 BILLION	$444 MILLION
Standard and Poor's	BBBq*	AA+	AA	AA+	BBBq*
Moody's	NR	NR	Aa1	NR	NR
Plan	50022,50021,50022	Golden Care Plus	P1-15203	LTC 4	11001
Age range	40-84	40-84	45-84	18-84	0-84
Benefit periods available	2,3,4, Lifetime	2,4, Lifetime (equivalent)	2,4,6, Lifetime	1,2,3,4, Lifetime	1,2,3,4, Lifetime
Minimum/Maximum Daily	$30-$200	$40-$200	$40-$250	$20-$250	$20-$200
Benefit amounts			By state	By State	
Elimination Periods	20,100	20,60	0,30,90	0,30,100	0,100
Must Elimination Period be repeated?	YES for each new condition or after 6 month break for same condition.	YES (after 6 month break)	YES for each new condition or after 6 month break for same condition.	only 30 day elimination, (after 6 month break) 100 days does not repeat	YES (after 6 month break)
Three Ways to Qualify for Benefits	YES	YES	YES	YES	YES
Covers all levels of care	YES	YES	YES	YES	YES
Guaranteed Renewable	YES	YES	YES	YES	YES
No prior hospital confinement	YES	YES	YES	YES	YES
Indemnity based	YES	NO	YES	YES	YES
Waiver of premium	YES - after 90 consecutive days of benefits	YES - after 60 consecutive days of confinement	YES - after 90 consecutive days of confinement (includes waiting period)	YES - after 90 days of benefits (waived for both spouses.)	YES - after 90 consecutive days of benefits
Compound Inflation (AP)	YES	YES	YES	YES	YES
Pre-existing Conditions	NONE	NONE	6 months if not disclosed on application	90 DAYS	NONE

*—"Solvency rating (Insurer has not paid S&P to assign a claims paying rating)"
(BP) Covered in base plan
(AP) Covered for an additional premium
(APC) Alternate Plan of Care
(ACF) Alternate Care Facility

Shaded areas indicate competitive disadvantage.

Additional Features

Company	AMEX	Bankers	CNA	PFL	Transport
Once in a lifetime elimination period	NO	NO	NO	YES 100 days	NO
Coordinates with Medicare	NO	YES	NO	NO	NO
Full Restoration of Benefits	NO	YES	YES	YES	YES
After benefit free		NO	NO	YES	NO
After treatment free		YES	YES or for new condition	NO	YES
Alternate Plan of Care (APC)	NO	YES (AP) Only with HHC rider	YES	YES	YES
Alternate care facility (ACF)	YES	NO	NO	Under (APC)	Not Routinely
APC/ACF Trigger	2 of 5 ADLs or Cognitive Impairment (ACF)	2 of 5 ADLs	In lieu of NH confinement	NH Confinement	In lieu of NH confinement
% of benefits available for APC/ACF	60% of Nursing home benefits (ACF)	100% of HHC benefits for APC	100% of Nursing Home Benefits	100% of Nursing Home Benefits	100% of Nursing Home Benefits
Survivorship Benefit	NO	YES	NO	YES	NO
Couples Waiver of Premium	NO	NO	NO	YES Couples premium is waived even if only one spouse is confined	NO
Couples Discount	NO	Preferred Rates	10%	Select Rates less 10%	10%
5% Simple Inflation Option	YES (AP)	NO	YES (AP)	YES (AP)	NO
Guaranteed Future Insurability when compound or simple inflation is not chosen.	NO	NO	NO	YES Additional premium charged only when exercised	NO
Prescription Drug Benefit	NO	NO	NO	YES	NO
Ambulance Benefit	NO	YES Pays $250 per trip, 4 per year.	NO	YES Pays $50 per trip, 3 per confinement	NO
Post Confinement Benefit	NO	YES	NO	NO	NO
Bed Reservation Benefit	YES	YES	YES	YES	NO
Respite Care	YES (HHC/AP)	YES (HHC/APC/AP)	YES (HHC/AP) (APC)	YES (APC)	YES (HHC/AP)
Equipment or Home Modification	YES (HHC/AP)	YES (HHC/AP)	YES (APC)	YES (APC)	YES (APC)
Return of Premium (AP)	YES	YES	YES	YES	YES
Premium Discount for Monthly PAC	NO	NO	NO	YES	NO

Home Health Care Rider Features

Company	AMEX	Bankers	CNA	PFL	Transport
Minimum/Maximum Daily Benefit Amounts	$30-$150	Same as nursing home	$40-$100	$20-$150 By State	$20-$100 (Must equal nursing home)
Elimination Period	20 days within 90 day period	Same as nursing home	5 visits (One visit after confinement)	10 or 30 days (0 or 20 after Confinement)	Same as nursing home
Benefit Period	1,2,3, Lifetime	250 days, 500 days (Equivalent) Lifetime	2,5, Lifetime	1,2,4, Lifetime	Same as nursing home
Access to Benefits	One ADL or cognitive impairment	Triple Trigger	Triple Trigger	Triple Trigger for the first 60 days of care	Triple Tripper
Indemnity Based	No	No	No	No	No
Coordinates with Medicare	No	Yes	Yes	Yes	No
Home Health Care Limitations	Medical Necessity is not a trigger to begin receiving Home Health Care Benefits.	Customer is forced to purchase higher amounts of Nursing Home benefits to receive sufficient amounts of Home Health Care benefits due to the 50% limitation on basic services.	Each 6 hours constitutes a new home health care visit (24 hrs. for respite care). 7 visits allowed weekly.	After 60 days, trigger is 2 of 5 ADLs	Must have 3 days of home health care in a calendar week to qualify for one day of home-maker services. This formula allows for only one day of homemaker services per week.
Are only those days for which an expense is incurred charged against the benefit period?	YES	YES	NO	YES	YES
Are Nursing Home and Home Health Care Benefits charged against the same Maximum?	NO	YES	NO	NO	YES
Benefits paid for:					
Advanced (skilled) services	100% of NHDB**	100% of NHDB**	100% of NHDB**	100% of NHDB**	80% of charge up to 100% of NHDB
Basic (custodial) services	100% of NHDB	50% of NHDB	80% of NHDB	80% of charge up to 100% of NHDB	80% of charge up to 100% of NHDB
Companion/homemaker services	100% of NHDB	50% of NHDB	80% of NHDB	80% of charge up to 100% of NHDB	80% of charge up to 100% of NHDB
Adult Day Care	100% of NHDB	25% of NHDB	80% of NHDB	80% of charge up to 100% of NHDB	80% of charge up to 50% of NHDB

**-NHDB = Nursing Home Daily Benefit

From LTC Consultants, compilers, "Long-Term Care Insurance Policy Comparison of Selected Policies," © 1993, LTC Consultants, a division of Shelton Marketing Services, Inc. Used by permission.

EXHIBIT 12
SOUTHERN BAPTIST RELATED HOUSING AND HEALTH CARE FACILITIES FOR THE AGING

Prepared by Arizona Baptist Retirement Centers, Inc.
December 14, 1994

ALABAMA

BAPTIST OAKS APARTMENTS
806 Government Street
Mobile, AL 36602
Phone: (205) 432-2312
Affiliation: Baptist Oaks, Inc.

BELL OAKS RETIREMENT COMMUNITY
3160 Bell Oaks Circle
Montgomery, AL 36116
Phone: (205) 281-4523
Affiliation: Baptist Health Services

EASTVIEW RETIREMENT CENTER
297 Sylvest Drive
Montgomery, AL 36117
Phone: (205) 279-7673
Affiliation: Alabama Baptist Retirement
Centers

KNOLLWOOD RETIREMENT CENTER
Rt. 4, Box 100
Roanoke, AL 36274
Phone: (205) 863-2415
Affiliation: Alabama Baptist Retirement
Centers

CLARA VERNER TOWER
501 River Road
Tuscaloosa, AL 35605
Phone: (205) 349-2202
Affiliation: Alabama Baptist Retirement
Centers

BAPTIST VILLAGE DOTHAN
3230 West Main Street
Dothan, AL 36301
Phone: (205) 793-3930
Affiliation: Alabama Baptist Retirement
Centers

CAPITOL HEIGHTS PLACE
135 South Panama Street
Montgomery, AL 36107
Phone: (205) 264-8378
Affiliation: Capitol Heights Baptist Church

HUTTO TOWER
3230 West Main Street
Dothan, AL 36301
Phone: (205) 793-3930
Affiliation: Alabama Baptist Retirement
Centers

PRINCETON TOWERS
909 Princeton Avenue, SW
Birmingham, AL 35211
Phone: (205) 783-3292
Affiliation: Baptist Hospitals Services
Corporation

ARIZONA

BAPTIST VILLAGE - NORTHEAST
PHOENIX
20802 North Cave Creek Road
Phoenix, AZ 85024
Phone: (602) 569-0508
Affiliation: Arizona Baptist Retirement
Centers, Inc.

BAPTIST VILLAGE - SUNRIDGE
12215 West Bell Road
Surprise, AZ 85374
Phone: (602) 583-5482
Affiliation: Arizona Baptist Retirement
Centers, Inc.

BAPTIST VILLAGE - YOUNGTOWN
11315 West Peoria Avenue
Youngtown, AZ 85363
Phone: (602) 972-2371
Affiliation: Arizona Baptist Retirement
Centers, Inc.

PARADISE VALLEY ESTATES
11645 North 25th Place
Phoenix, AZ 85028
Phone: (602) 788-8090
Affiliation: Arizona Baptist Retirement
Centers, Inc.

BAPTIST VILLAGE - THUNDERBIRD
13617 North 55th Avenue
Glendale, AZ 85304
Phone: (602) 938-5500
Affiliation: Arizona Baptist Retirement
Centers, Inc.

CALIFORNIA

FICKETT TOWER
14801 Sherman Way
Van Nuys, CA 91405
Phone: (818) 988-8628
Affiliation: First Baptist Church Van Nuys

PARK PACIFIC TOWER
714 Pacific Avenue
Long Beach, CA 90813
Phone: (310) 435-1803
Affiliation: South Hills Baptist Church

DISTRICT OF COLUMBIA

THOMAS HOUSE
1330 Massachusetts Avenue, NW
Washington, DC 20005
Phone: (202) 628-3844
Affiliation: Baptist Senior Adult Ministries
of the Washington Area, Inc.

FLORIDA

BAPTIST MANOR
10095 Hillview Road
Pensacola, FL 32514
Phone: (904) 479-4000
Affiliation: Baptist Health Care

BAPTIST TOWERS OF JACKSONVILLE
1400 LeBarron Street
Jacksonville, FL 36602
Phone: (904) 398-3406
Affiliation: Baptist Towers, Inc.

CENTRAL MANOR APARTMENTS
136 Fairview
Daytona Beach, FL 32018
Phone: (904) 255-2622
Affiliation: Central Baptist Church

FLORIDA BAPTIST RETIREMENT CENTERS
P.O. Box 460
Vero Beach, FL 32961
Phone: (407) 567-5248
Affiliation: Florida Baptist Family Ministries

PENSACOLA VILLAGE
1700 "L" Street
Pensacola, FL 32514
Phone: (904) 433-5035
Affiliation: Baptist Health Care

TAMPA BAPTIST MANOR
215 Grand Central Avenue
Tampa, FL 33606
Phone: (813) 253-2868
Affiliation: First Baptist Church, Tampa

BAPTIST TOWERS
414 East Pine
Orlando, FL 32801
Phone: (407) 841-7207
Affiliation: First Baptist Housing, Inc.

CASA DE PALMA
302 East Palm Avenue
Tampa, FL 33602
Phone: (813) 223-2686
Affiliation: Casa De Palma, Inc.

COLLEGE PARK TOWERS
5200 Eggleston Avenue
Orlando, FL 32801
Phone: (407) 291-1542
Affiliation: College Park Baptist Church

PALM AVENUE BAPTIST TOWER
215 East Palm Avenue
Tampa, FL 33602
Phone: (813) 223-2686
Affiliation: Palm Avenue Baptist Church

PLANT CITY TOWERS
103 Mahoney Street
Plant City, FL 33566
Phone: (813) 752-5116
Affiliation: Baptist Towers of Plant City, Inc.

WHITE SANDS MANOR
40 Windham Avenue, SE
Ft. Walton Beach, FL 32548
Phone: (904) 244-7162
Affiliation: Northwest Florida Non-Profit
Retirement Housing, Inc.

GEORGIA

ADULT DAY CARE
300 Boulevard NE
Atlanta, GA 30312
Phone: (404) 653-3591
Affiliation: Georgia Baptist Medical Center

BAPTIST VILLAGE
P.O. Drawer 1100
Waycross, GA 31501
Phone: (912) 283-7050
Affiliation: Georgia Baptist Convention

CLAIRMONT OAKS
441 Clairmont Avenue
Decatur, GA 30030
Phone: (404) 378-8887
Affiliation: Clairmont Oaks, Inc.

KING'S BRIDGE RETIREMENT CENTER
3055 Briarcliff Road
Atlanta, GA 30329
Phone: (404) 321-0263
Affiliation: King's Bridge Retirement
Center, Inc.

PACES FERRY APARTMENTS
374 East Paces Ferry Road, NE
Atlanta, GA 30305
Phone: (404) 233-4421
Affiliation: Georgia Baptist Homes

BAPTIST INN RETIREMENT HOME
1424 Hudson Bridge Road
Stockbridge, GA 30281
Phone: (404) 474-6416
Affiliation: Georgia Baptist Homes, Inc.

BRIARCLIFF OAKS
2982 Briarcliff Road, NE
Atlanta, GA 30329
Phone: (404) 634-3263
Affiliation: Clairmont Oaks, Inc.

HARVEST HEIGHTS
3200 Panthersville Road
Decatur, GA 30034
Phone: (404) 243-8460
Affiliation: Georgia Baptist Medical Center

NEWTON HOUSE SUB-ACUTE
REHABILITATION
320 Parkway Drive
Atlanta, GA 30312
Phone: (404) 653-8197
Affiliation: Georgia Baptist Medical Center

HAWAII

HALE HO'OLAI SENIOR DAY CARE CENTER
2305 University Avenue
Honolulu, HI 96822
Phone: (808) 955-4753
Affiliation: University Avenue Baptist Church

KENTUCKY

BAPTIST CONVALESCENT CENTER, INC.
120 Main Street
Newport, KY 41071
Phone: (606) 581-1938
Affiliation: Northern Kentucky Baptist
Association

BAPTIST TOWER
1014 South Second Street
Louisville, KY 40203
Phone: (502) 587-6632
Affiliation: Walnut Street Baptist Church

LOUISIANA

BAPTIST RETIREMENT CENTER OF ARCADIA
1109 6th Street
Arcadia, LA 71001
Phone: (318) 263-9581
Affiliation: Louisiana Baptist Convention

MARYLAND

UNIVERSITY FELLOWSHIP ADULT DAY
CARE CENTER
3515 Campus Drive
College Park, MD 20740
Phone: (301) 422-7970
Affiliation: Baptist Senior Adult Ministries
of Metropolitan Washington Area, Inc.

BRENTWOOD ADULT DAY CARE
CENTER
3601 Taylor Street
Brentwood, MD 20722
Phone: (301) 699-0851
Affiliation: Baptist Senior Adult Ministries
of the Metropolitan Washington Area, Inc.

BAPTIST HOME OF
MARYLAND/DELAWARE
10729 Park Heights Avenue
Owings Mills, MD 21117
Phone: (410) 484-3321
Affiliation: Baptist Convention of
Maryland and Delaware

MISSOURI

THE BAPTIST HOME
P.O. Box 87, Hwy. 72 East
Ironton, MO 63650
Phone: (314) 546-7429
Affiliation: The Baptist Home, Inc.

THE BAPTIST HOME - CHILLICOTHE
P.O. Box 920, Hwy. 65 North
Chillicothe, MO 64601
Phone: (816) 646-6219
Affiliation: The Baptist Home, Inc.

PLEASANT VALLEY MANOR
305 Hampton
West Plains, MO 65775
Phone: (417) 257-0179
Affiliation: West Vue Home, Inc.

PLEASANT VALLEY VILLAGE
305 Hampton
West Plains, MO 65775
Phone: (417) 257-0179
Affiliation: West Vue Home, Inc.

WEST VUE APARTMENTS
907 Kentucky
West Plains, MO 65775
Phone: (417) 256-1292
Affiliation: West Vue Home, Inc.

WEST VUE HOME
909 Kentucky
West Plains, MO 65775
Phone: (417) 256-2152
Affiliation: West Vue Home, Inc.

NORTH CAROLINA

BROOKRIDGE RETIREMENT COMMUNITY
1199 Hayes Forest Drive
Winston-Salem, NC 27106
Phone: (919) 759-1044
Affiliation: Baptist Retirement Homes
of North Carolina, Inc.

CROSS ROAD VILLAGE
1302 Old Cox Road
Asheboro, NC 27203
Phone: (919) 629-7811
Affiliation: Cross Road Village, Inc.

TAYLOR HOUSE
407 Palmer Street
Albemarle, NC 28002
Phone: (704) 982-4217
Affiliation: Baptist Retirement Homes
of North Carolina, Inc.

THE CROSS ROAD REST &
RETIREMENT CENTER
1302 Old Cox Road
Asheboro, NC 27203
Phone: (919) 629-7811
Affiliation: The Cross Road Rest &
Retirement Center, Inc.

HAMILTON BAPTIST HOME
P.O. Box 220, Railroad Street
Hamilton, NC 27840
Phone: (919) 798-5901
Affiliation: Baptist Retirement Homes
of North Carolina, Inc.

WESTERN NORTH CAROLINA
BAPTIST HOME
213 Richmond Hill Drive
Asheville, NC 28806
Phone: (704) 254-9675
Affiliation: Baptist Retirement Homes
of North Carolina, Inc.

OKLAHOMA

ADA BAPTIST VILLAGE
3501 Oakridge Boulevard
Ada, OK 74820
Phone: (405) 332-6004
Affiliation: Baptist General Convention
of Oklahoma

CLEVELAND BAPTIST VILLAGE
1001 Baptist Village Drive
Cleveland, OK 74020
Phone: (918) 358-2575
Affiliation: Baptist General Convention
of Oklahoma

LACKEY MANOR NURSING HOME
9700 Mashburn Boulevard
Oklahoma City, OK 73162
Phone: (405) 721-2466
Affiliation: Baptist General Convention
of Oklahoma

**OKLAHOMA CITY BAPTIST
RETIREMENT CENTER**
9700 Mashburn Boulevard
Oklahoma City, OK 73162
Phone: (405) 721 2466
Affiliation: Baptist General Convention
of Oklahoma

**RAYOLA BAPTIST COMMUNITY-
EVERGREEN CARE CENTER**
12600 East 73rd Street
Owasso, OK 74055
Phone: (918) 272-8007
Affiliation: Baptist General Convention
of Oklahoma

BAPTIST RETIREMENT CENTER
7410 North 127 East Avenue
Owasso, OK 74055
Phone: (918) 272-2281
Affiliation: Baptist General Convention
of Oklahoma

HUGO BAPTIST RETIREMENT CENTER
P.O. Drawer 608
1200 West Finley
Hugo, OK 74743
Phone: (405) 326-8383
Affiliation: Baptist General Convention
of Oklahoma

MADILL BAPTIST VILLAGE
Rt. 3, Box 101
Madill, OK 72446
Phone: (405) 564-3776
Affiliation: Baptist General Convention
of Oklahoma

OKMULGEE BAPTIST VILLAGE
1500 West 6th
Okmulgee, OK 74447
Phone: (918) 756-5377
Affiliation: Baptist General Convention
of Oklahoma

RIVERMONT AT THE TRAILS
800 Canadian Trails Drive
Norman, OK 73072
Phone: (405) 360-0606
Affiliation: Arizona Baptist Retirement
Centers, Inc.

SOUTH CAROLINA

MARTHA FRANKS BAPTIST
RETIREMENT CENTER
1 Martha Franks Drive
Laurens, SC 29360
Phone: (803) 984-4541
Affiliation: South Carolina Baptist
Ministries for the Aging, Inc.

BETHEA BAPTIST RETIREMENT
COMMUNITY & HEALTH CARE CENTER
P.O. Box 4000
Darlington, SC 29532
Phone: (803) 393-2867
Affiliation: South Carolina Baptist
Ministries for the Aging, Inc.

ROLLING GREEN VILLAGE
1 Hoke Smith Boulevard
Greenville, SC 29615
Phone: (803) 297-0558
Affiliation: Greenville Baptist Retirement
Community

TENNESSEE

BAPTIST HEALTH CARE CENTER
700 Williams Ferry Road
Lenoir City, TN 37771
Phone: (615) 986-3583
Affiliation: Tennessee Baptist Adult
Homes, Inc.

DEER LAKE RETIREMENT VILLAGE
368 Deer Lake Drive
Nashville, TN 37221
Phone: (615) 646-3882
Affiliation: Tennessee Baptist Adult
Homes, Inc.

BAPTIST VILLAGE OF JOHNSON CITY
Cherokee Road
Johnson City, TN 37601
Phone: (615) 371-2050
Affiliation: Tennessee Baptist Adult
Homes, Inc.

TEXAS

BAPTIST MEMORIALS CENTER
902-903 North Main - Box 5561
San Angelo, TX 76902
Phone: (915) 655-7391
Affiliation: Baptist General Convention
of Texas

BUCKNER RETIREMENT VILLAGE
4800 Samuell Boulevard
Dallas, TX 75228
Phone: (214) 381-2171
Affiliation: Buckner Baptist
Benevolences, Inc.

BUCKNER VILLA RETIREMENT VILLAGE
1001 East Braker Lane
Austin, TX 78753
Phone: (512) 836-1515
Affiliation: Buckner Baptist
Benevolences, Inc.

**HENDRICK RESIDENTIAL
RETIREMENT CENTER**
1102 North 19th
Abilene, TX 79601
Phone: (915) 670-2508
Affiliation: Hendrick Medical Development

MONTE SIESTA NURSING CENTER
4700 Dudmar
Austin, TX 79746
Phone: (512) 892-1131
Affiliation: Buckner Baptist
Benevolences, Inc.

BUCKNER BAPTIST HAVEN
12601 Memorial Drive
Houston, TX 77024-4892
Phone: (713) 465-3406
Affiliation: Buckner Baptist
Benevolences, Inc.

BUCKNER RETIREMENT VILLAGE
7111 Alabama
El Paso, TX 79904
Phone: (915) 751-1007
Affiliation: Buckner Baptist
Benevolences, Inc.

**GOLDEN PALMS RETIREMENT &
HEALTH CENTER**
2101 Treasure Hills Boulevard
Harlingen, TX 78550
Phone: (210) 421-4653, (210) 421-1500
Affiliation: Golden Palms Retirement &
Health Center

MESA SPRINGS
7171 Buffalo Gap Road
Abilene, TX 79606
Phone: (915) 692-8080
Affiliation: Mesa Springs Retirement
Village, Inc.

**PARK PLACE TOWERS AND THE
CONTINENTAL**
1300 South Harrison
Amarillo, TX 79101
Phone: (806) 376-1177
Affiliation: High Plains Baptist Hospital

VIRGINIA

CULPEPER BAPTIST RETIREMENT COMMUNITY
P.O. Box 191
Culpeper, VA 22701
Phone: (703) 825-2411
Affiliation: Virginia Baptist Homes, Inc.

THE EMILY GREEN HOME & MORAN RIVERVIEW HOUSE
Westmoreland Avenue
Portsmouth, VA 23707
Phone: (804) 399-3442
Affiliation: Portsmouth Baptist Association

LAKEWOOD MANOR BAPTIST RETIREMENT COMMUNITY
1900 Lauderdale Drive
Richmond, VA 23233
Phone: (804) 740-2900
Affiliation: Virginia Baptist Homes, Inc.

NEWPORT NEWS BAPTIST RETIREMENT COMMUNITY
955 Harpersville Road
Newport News, VA 23601
Phone: (804) 599-4376
Affiliation: Virginia Baptist Homes, Inc.

WASHINGTON

PARKLAND TERRACE
3133 Maryland Street
Longview, WA 98632
Phone: (206) 423-1150
Affiliation: First Baptist Ministries, Inc.

WESTGATE TERRACE
2024 Tibbetts Drive
Longview, WA 98632
Phone: (206) 425-0590
Affiliation: First Baptist Ministries, Inc.